Plant Location
Decisions of Foreign
Manufacturing Investors

Research for Business Decisions, No. 17

Other Titles in This Series

Plant Location
Decisions of Foreign
Manufacturing Investors

by
Hsin-Min Tong

RESEARCH PRESS

338613

Produced and distributed by
University Microfilms International
Ann Arbor, Michigan 48106

Library of Congress Cataloging in Publication Data

Tong, Hsin-Min, 1947-
 Plant location decisions of foreign manufacturing
investors in the U. S.

  (Research for business decisions ; no. 17)
  Bibliography: p.
  Includes index.
  1. Industries, Location of—United States. 2. Factories—
United States—Location. 3. Investments, Foreign—United
States. 4. United States—Manufactures. I. Title. II. Series.
HC110.D5T66   658.2'1'0973   79-22203
ISBN 0-8357-1056-4

TABLE OF CONTENTS

CONTENTS

ILLUSTRATIONS

TABLES

TABLES

TABLES

TABLES

TABLES

ACKNOWLEDGMENTS

I would like to acknowledge with sincere gratitude the contributions to this study made by my professors in the College of Business Administration at the University of Nebraska-Lincoln. I am especially thankful to the following persons: Dean Gary Schwendiman for his assistance in writing a cover letter used in the mail survey; Professor C. K. Walter, chairman of my entire doctoral program, for his invaluable advice, willingness to help, and patience; and Professors Richard J. Schonberger, William W. Curtis, and John J. Brasch for their continuing guidance in planning the study and in solving special problems throughout the research endeavor.

Mr. W. T. Wheeler, of Nebraska State Economic Development Department, deserves special recognition for his tremendous help in compiling the mailing list. Special thanks are extended to many directors of the fifty state economic development agencies who supplied the current list of names and addresses of foreign manufacturers, and to those foreign manufacturers who provided empirical information.

Finally, I wish to express my deepest appreciation to my parents, sisters, brothers, brother-in-law, and many friends for their continuous understanding and encouragement.

ACKNOWLEDGMENTS

CHAPTER I

INTRODUCTION

BACKGROUND

Investment has been defined as the commitment of money or capital for the purpose of gaining profitable returns.[1] From the point of view of the United States as a nation, foreign investment can be classified as shown in Figure 1-1.[2] This book was an investigation of plant location decisions of inward foreign manufacturing investors in the United States.[3] The primary objectives of this study were threefold: (1) to identify the factors which have important influence on non-American manufacturing investors in making locational choices for their plants in the U.S.; (2) to supply useful information to communities in the U.S. for improving their investment climates; and (3) to facilitate the exchange of opinions and experiences of choosing plant locations among foreign manufacturing investors in the U.S.

According to the U.S. Department of Commerce, non-Americans had 26.5 billion dollars' worth of direct investment in the U.S. as of 1974, of which about one-third was engaged in some form of manufacturing.[4] It is generally agreed that the establishment of foreign manufacturing plants in the U.S. is helpful to the economic development of the U.S.[5] The rationale behind this kind of thinking is that:

1. Foreign manufacturing investments would increase the national employment level; Walter E. Greene, in his book *Plant Location Factors*, said:

   > New industry, preferably some type of manufacturing, would help diversify and widen the employment opportunities. For each 100 new factory workers a city requires 110 more households, 4 more retail establishments, 107 more passenger cars and 75 more workers to support factory workers.[6]

2. Foreign manufacturing investments have a positive impact, due to the capital inflow, on the U.S. balance of international payments.
3. Foreign manufacturing investments increase the total output of goods, which would reduce the inflationary pressure.
4. Foreign manufacturing investments induce transfers of technology from abroad, which can raise the efficiency of production to this nation.[7]

The relevant literature has shown over and over that choosing a plant location is a managerial decision of utmost importance to almost all kinds of

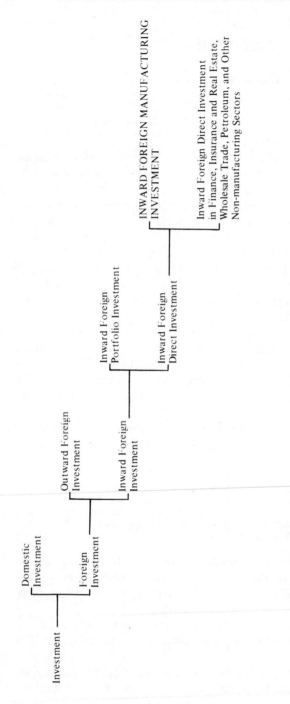

FIGURE 1-1. CLASSIFICATION OF INVESTMENT[a]

[a] Adapted from U.S. Congress, House, *International Investment Uncertainty*. 94th Cong., 2nd sess. (Washington: U.S. Government Printing Office, 1977), pp. 17-19.

manufacturing firms.[8] F.E. LeVan, a senior engineer for DuPont who has played a key role in many plant location projects, clearly expressed this point by saying:

> . . . the problem of plant site selection . . . is one of the most critical decisions that industrial management has to make in considering a new plant . . . . Competition in industry and rising costs have made it more and more imperative that all items affecting investment and cost of operation be thoroughly analyzed and the plant located where they can be held to a minimum . . . . Operating defects usually can be corrected at comparatively low cost, but faults of location are forever carried as a manufacturing burden.[9]

The term "foreign manufacturing investors" in this study refers to manufacturing firms which have at least one plant in the U.S. and of whose ownership 10 percent or more belongs to non-Americans.[10] The use of "10 percent" as a cut-off point here is consistent with the definition of foreign direct investment currently adopted by the U.S. Department of Commerce.[11] "Foreign manufacturers" is another term which is used interchangeably with foreign manufacturing investors in this work.

STATEMENT OF THE PROBLEM

This study examined four problems regarding plant location decisions of foreign manufacturing investors in the U.S. These four problems follow.

Problem 1

What is the importance of various plant location factors in the eyes of foreign manufacturing investors in the U.S.?

Discussion. A thorough literature review provided a list of 32 plant location factors which might have influenced plant location decisions of foreign manufacturing investors in the U.S.[12] The problem raised here is distinguishing those more important plant location factors from the less important ones. To explore the relationships between various characteristics of foreign manufacturing investors and the relative importance of plant location factors, the following five sub-questions were posed:

Problem 1a. Does the importance of a plant location factor vary by category of products produced by foreign manufacturers in the U.S.?

Problem 1b. Does the importance of a plant location factor vary by employee size of foreign manufacturing plants in the U.S.?

Problem 1c. Does the importance of a plant location factor vary by location within the U.S. of the foreign manufacturing plants?

Problem 1d. Does the importance of a plant location factor vary by degree of foreign ownership of manufacturing firms in the U.S.?

Problem 1e. Does the importance of a plant location factor vary by national origin of foreign manufacturing investors in the U.S.?

These five sub-questions are designed to be statistically tested. The detailed discussions about them will come in the hypotheses section in this chapter.

Problem 2

What are the basic "dimensions" or "groupings" underlying this relatively large number of plant location factors?

Discussion. Whenever there is a relatively large number of variables which affect an individual's or an institution's behavior, it is often appropriate to find out the basic dimensions underlying these variables.[13] In social psychologist Dr. Jean Stoetzel's words, ". . . there is a need for a deeper knowledge of their (the relatively large number of variables') roots."[14] Frederick Williams further explained, ". . . (this is) a more economical way to characterize the behavior that we are studying."[15] The data collected for the first problem were reanalyzed to give an answer to this question.[16]

Problem 3

From what sources do foreign manufacturing investors in the U.S. get information in order to decide in which community to locate their plant?

Discussion. How can economic development organizations in the U.S. effectively disseminate information to prospective foreign manufacturing investors? To answer this question, it is necessary to find out from where the foreign manufacturing investors get their information in regard to making plant location decisions in the U.S. The findings from this problem can enhance the communication between the economic development organizations and foreign manufacturing investors.

Problem 4

What percentage and what kinds of foreign manufacturers in the U.S. have not made a plant location decision and why?

Discussion. Previous studies have shown that certain foreign manufacturers in the U.S. did not make any plant location decision, but they do have a plant.[17] This problem tries to determine how prevalent this situation is, what characteristics this special group of foreign manufacturers possesses and why this kind of thing happened.

Since the basic purpose of this study is to supply useful information to improve the investment climate at the community level, the empirical questioning of this study has its focus on communities, rather than on regions or on specific plant sites.

JUSTIFICATION OF THE STUDY

Although the history of foreign manufacturing investment in the U.S. can be traced back to the very early times of this nation's foundation, the great interest in it did not arise until recent years.[18] There is no mandatory registration required for foreign manufacturing investment in this country. At the present time, very limited empirical data exist on this subject.[19] In a recent study, published in 1974, on foreign direct investment in the U.S., Simon Webley wrote:

> One of the difficulties in evaluating foreign direct investment in the United States is the lack of accurate data on where it is located, how much is invested and in what industries. Furthermore, little information is available on what happens once an initial investment has been made—does it expand by acquisition or by building new or extending existing plants? Nor are there figures for employment in foreign-owned factories and offices.[20]

The need for more factual information about foreign manufacturing investments in the U.S. appears obvious.

An extensive review of literature concerning plant location decisions revealed that almost all of the existing articles and studies were on either the U.S. or foreign nation's domestic manufacturing investment. After interviewing more than 30 executives of foreign manufacturers currently operating in the U.S., Tom Foster, the associate editor of *Distribution Worldwide,* stated:

> . . . while the rationale for foreign companies coming to the U.S. is clear, the criteria each company uses to choose an industrial site are not so obvious. . . . We found that foreign companies locating here have a different set of priorities for site selection than their American counterparts. The traditional importance the U.S. shipper gives to freight costs, proximity to markets and other practical considerations is not shared by the foreign company. Instead, strategic matters such as long-term availability of raw materials, access to world markets and room for expansion seem to be prime considerations for site location by foreign companies.[21]

To be sure that no study of the same nature and extent was done in the past, inquiring letters were sent to the fifty states' economic development agencies, the U.S. Department of Commerce, and some relevant private research institutions.[22] The replies indicated that such a study was worthwhile and well justified.

MODEL OF THE PLANT-LOCATION-DECISION PROCESS

A model is a replica of some real system or process. It integrates elements into a meaningful whole. As such, it offers a valuable reference framework for research, in which the relevant variables are identified, and the interrelationships among these variables specified. There are many types of models. The one to be discussed in this section is, according to modeling terminology, a "logic-flow model," which presents a graphical representation of a process.[23]

Combining the concepts of general decision making and international business decision making with Professor Donald J. Bowersox' ideas of plant location procedure, a model of plant-location-decision process was constructed.[24] This is a model developed for foreign manufacturing investors in the U.S. and is used only as a conceptual framework to bring together the various pieces of this research.

The process that foreign manufacturing investors move through in choosing a plant location in the U.S. is conceptualized as a stage process. It consists of six stages: need and expectation, decision of investment, plant analysis, field analysis, decision of plant location, and confirmation. Figure 1-2 shows the model and the relevant variables which influence the stages. Following is a discussion of each of these stages.

Need and expectation

This stage may begin under various situations. For example, if a foreign businessman encounters such problems as high U.S. tariffs and high transportation costs, he would probably feel the need to set up production operations within the U.S. A typical case of this kind is Toshiba, a major Japanese electronics firm, which recently announced plans to build a TV manufacturing plant in the U.S.[25] Some foreign investors come to the U.S. not because they need to solve any problems, but because they want to gain certain things which otherwise are not readily accessible to them. B.W. Industries, an Australian manufacturer of concrete pumps, set up its plant near Seattle, Washington, in 1975. Its president, Peter Wilton, explained, "Being here gives us access to their (Boeing Company's) suppliers and to the engineering know-how we couldn't get in Australia."[26] The change of environmental variables like the devaluations of the U.S. dollar, the awareness of the political stability of the U.S., and the foreign firm's own conditions like the level of technology may also make foreign businessmen start thinking of building plants in the U.S. A complete literature review about the reasons foreign investors have come to the U.S. is presented in Chapter 2.

**FIGURE 1-2 MODEL OF PLANT-LOCATION-DECISION PROCESS FOR
FOREIGN MANUFACTURING INVESTORS IN THE U.S.**

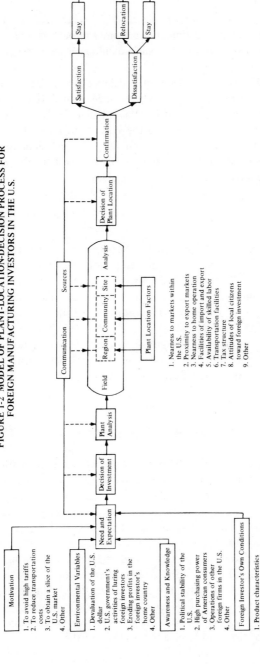

Decision of investment

At this stage, if the decision involves a big foreign firm or a huge investment, there is often a long lead time and a team approach is used.[27] The final investment decision together with company manufacturing strategy and policy is usually made by the top management.[28]

Sometimes the investment decision is delayed because of a single factor. Kikkoman, a Japanese manufacturer of soy sauce with 300 years of history, started exporting to the U.S. market in 1957. William E. Nelson, the manager of Kikkoman's plant located in Walworth, Wisconsin, said, "It became clear that it was inefficient to import grain from the U.S. and then to export the finished product back to the U.S. . . but it wasn't until recently that the U.S. sales volume became large enough to warrant a plant here."[29]

Plant analysis

Once the decision of investment has been made, the present and potential market locations and the approximate quantity of goods to be shipped need to be determined. The plant designers then should spell out a set of location specifications, including such items as the amount and skill of labor required, the availability and cost of transportation facilities, the utility requirements, the space needed, and so forth.

Stressing the existence of alternative methods of production, Ronald H. Hermone suggested that more than one set of location specifications should be developed.[30] According to Bowersox, a detailed analysis of competitive forces and intangible factors should also be completed in this stage.[31]

Field analysis

The formal and active search for a plant location starts with this stage. The result from the plant-analysis stage serves as both a starting point and an evaluation criterion for the field analysis. Field analysis is usually performed on three levels: region, community, and site. Occasionally, it includes only two levels, region and community, because there may exist only one suitable plant site in a small community.[32]

The basic information about region and community are available in such magazines as *Plant Location* and *Site Selection Handbook*.[33] In order to get detailed data or gain some insights into the matter, the plant locators, however, have to contact the relevant people or organizations by mail or telephone, or visit the prospective places in person. Some specialists have recommended the use of aerial photos at the third level, site selection, of the stage.

Plant location factors are those elemental forces which affect plant location decisions of manufacturing investors. A list of plant location factors which may be important to foreign manufacturing investors in the U.S. has been developed at the end of Chapter 2, based on a thorough literature review. Examples are nearness to markets within the U.S., proximity to export markets, nearness to home operation, facilities of import and export, attitudes of government officials, and availabilities of skilled labor.[34]

Decision of plant location

Only after the above four stages have been gone through are the manufacturing investors ready to make a plant location decision. The information collected in the stage of field analysis makes it possible to compare different alternatives at the region, community, and site levels. Some of these comparisons are obvious and simple, but some others are fairly complicated and time consuming. The decision of a plant location is really a compromise among various location factors. In short, this stage involves certain comparison and elimination activities which lead to the final decision of a plant site.

Confirmation

This is the final stage. After a plant location decision has been made, the manufacturing investor may seek more information to evaluate how good or bad his plant location decision was. Or, he may wait and base his evaluation on later business operations. As shown in Figure 1-2, the output of confirmation could be either satisfaction or dissatisfaction. If the manufacturing investor is satisfied, most likely he would stay where he is. Dissatisfaction with the plant location, however, can be a serious problem. Under this situation, the manufacturing investor may reverse his previous decision or relocate his plant.

Theoretically, the confirmation stage can last forever. A once-satisfied manufacturing investor may become dissatisfied at a later time due to the changes of such variables as production technology developments, market shifts, and labor attitudes.

Communication sources

These are people or places from where relevant plant location information is obtained. Jeffrey S. Arpan and David A. Ricks found that other business firms, investment missions, state agencies, and the U.S. Department of Commerce were the communication sources most frequently used by foreign manufacturing investors in the U.S.[35]

HYPOTHESES

Corresponding to the five sub-questions listed under problem statement one, five sets of hypotheses were designed to be statistically tested. They are:

Hypothesis set 1

The importance of a plant location factor varies by category of products produced by foreign manufacturers in the U.S.

Discussion. The foreign manufacturers were divided, according to the category of their plant's major product(s), into eleven groups.[36] Since it generally requires different combinations of production factors to produce different categories of products, a reasonable conjecture is that plants producing different categories of products would emphasize different plant location factors.

Hypothesis set 2

The importance of a plant location factor varies by employee size of foreign manufacturing plants in the U.S.

Discussion. The foreign manufacturers were divided, according to the employee size of their plants, into three groups. Employee size here is used as an indicator of plant size. Since plants of different sizes generally involve different amounts or levels of production factors, it is even not unusual that drastically different manufacturing processes are used; it is, therefore, possible that plants with different employee sizes would emphasize different plant location factors.

Hypothesis set 3

The importance of a plant location factor varies by location within the U.S. of the foreign manufacturing plants.

Discussion. This hypothesis set was tested at both state and regional levels.[37] Each states or region has its own advantages and disadvantages in terms of natural and human-created environment. It is likely that plants were located in different states or regions due to the foreign manufacturing investors' emphases on different plant location factors, which are really part of the natural and human-created environment. At the state level, only the data from those foreign manufacturers whose plants are located in one of the 12 more important states, in terms of number of existing foreign manufacturing plants in a state, were used in testing this set of hypotheses.[38] At the regional level, the data from all 50 states were used, and the nation was divided into nine regions according to the standard breakdown adopted by the U.S. Department of Commerce.[39]

Hypothesis set 4

The importance of a plant location factor varies by degree of foreign ownership in manufacturing firms in the U.S.

Discussion. The foreign manufacturers were divided, according to the degree of foreign ownership, into four groups. There is a possibility that these four groups of foreign manufacturing investors would stress dissimilar plant location factors because different degrees of foreign ownership mean different levels of interest, control, and influence foreign investors have in a company.

Hypothesis set 5

The importance of a plant location factor varies by national origin of foreign manufacturing investors in the U.S.

Discussion. Investors from different countries have different social, cultural, political, and economic backgrounds. Their values, beliefs, attitudes, motivations, preferences, and habits are rarely the same. Therefore, their emphases on plant location factors and behaviors in choosing plant locations might be different. Only the data from those foreign manufacturers whose national origin is one of the eight highest foreign-manufacturing-investing countries in the U.S. were used in testing this set of hypotheses.[40]

Each of the hypothesis sets 1, 2, 4, and 5 includes 32 hypotheses, one for each plant location factor. Hypothesis set 3 was tested at two levels, state and region, and therefore has 64 hypotheses. All together, 192 hypotheses were tested.

SCOPE AND LIMITATIONS

This study was an investigation of the location selections of foreign plants which manufacture goods in the U.S. Therefore, the findings of this study may not be directly applicable to the following situations: (1) retail business locations, office locations, and warehouse locations; (2) American firms; and (3) foreign firms in other countries.

The focus of the empirical questioning of this study was on selecting a particular community, not a region or a plant site, in which to place a plant. Hence, those who work at the regional level or are concerned with specific plant sites should read this research report cautiously. The relative importance of plant location factors may very likely change when the consideration level is changed from community to region or site.

The "General Instructions" of the questionnaire requested that it be answered by an executive who either participated in or has knowledge of the company's plant location decisions in the U.S. To the extent that this instruction was followed, the empirical findings are reliable. However, the responses did not indicate who actually filled out the questionnaire.

Although many previous location studies limited themselves to a specific time period, say from 1963 to 1972, this investigation chose not to do so. The reason of not setting this limitation was to get an entire picture of this issue.

POTENTIAL CONTRIBUTIONS

The potential contributions of the present study are threefold. It may be useful to government officials, foreign manufacturing investors, and academicians. State and local officials may particularly find the results of this study useful in their efforts to identify and influence desirable types of foreign manufacturing investors to locate production plants in their states and communities. Professor Joseph A. Russell, the former Head of the Department of Geography of the University of Illinois, once commented on the subject of plant location:

> . . . Successful merging of the interests of industry and community is one of the most critical problems facing our dynamic industrial scene. It requires the care and understanding of both the industry seeking a new location and the community seeking a new industry . . . to attract an industry that will fail is worse than getting none at all.[41]

Foreign manufacturing investors may be interested in the findings of this study because the plant location decision is absolutely important to any manufacturing firm. Sten Soderman spoke out clearly:

> An entrepreneur's choice of location for his firm is probably one of the most important decisions he will ever make. It fixes the location from which he is henceforth obliged to purchase his raw materials, his semi-finished products and his energy. It establishes the size and quality of the workforce available to him and, in some cases, it defines the markets in which he can sell his products. What is more, once the decision is implemented there can be no turning back. The financial implications of moving a second time will, in almost all cases, force him to stay where he is.[42]

Wording vividly, William B. Speir said, "Selecting a plant site can be compared to selecting a wife. While it is possible to change later on, the change may be both expensive and unpleasant. Naturally, it is better to make a good choice the first time."[43] Due to their unfamiliarity with situations in the U.S., the coming foreign manufacturing investors very likely hope to know the opinions of other foreign manufacturing investors who have already had some experience in choosing plant locations in the U.S. This is partially evidenced by the words of Mr. Hunder A. Poole, Chief of International Section of North Carolina Department of Commerce:

For the past nineteen years it has been my personal privilege to have worked with perhaps as many as one thousand, both domestic and foreign, industries. It is from this experience that my conclusion is made that foreign companies have a tendency to be far more thorough and require approximately three times the amount of research and work as does its domestic counterpart.[44]

Academicians who are interested in foreign investment or plant location decisions, or both, may find this study valuable. The findings fill one of the knowledge gaps in this area. In this research, a conceptual model was constructed. Although not empirically tested, this model has the potential to lead to further development and refinement of plant-location-decision theory.

ORGANIZATION

There are five chapters in this book. Chapter 1 started with a discussion of the general background, and followed with specific problem statements, justification of the study, the model of plant-location-decision process for foreign manufacturing investors in the U.S., hypotheses, scope and limitations, and potential contributions. A review of the literature related to foreign investment and plant location in general and plant locations of foreign manufacturing investors in the U.S. in particular is presented in Chapter 2.

The research method, the development of a questionnaire, the pretest, the analysis of returns of the full-scale study, and the data analysis scheme are described in Chapter 3. The general characteristics of the responding foreign manufacturing investors, the descriptive findings, and the results of hypotheses tests constitute the material of Chapter 4. The fifth chapter includes a summary of the research, conclusions, practical implications, and suggestions for further study in this area.

CHAPTER II

LITERATURE REVIEW

The single most important feature of this study is that it collects data from a special group of respondents—the foreign manufacturing investors in the U.S. Therefore, the literature about foreign investment is reviewed first. After that follows a survey of related location theories and empirical studies. A basic purpose of this chapter is to develop an adequate list of plant location factors with regard to foreign manufacturing investments in the U.S.

FOREIGN INVESTMENT IN THE U.S.

"Foreign investment" is not a new term in the United States. As Professors John C. Clendenin and George A. Christy pointed out, "For the past 50 years American investors have paid increasing attention to opportunities outside the boundaries of the United States."[1] The two major reasons accounting for this situation were: (1) the capital supply in the U.S. grew at such a rapid rate that the interest returns on foreign securities became higher than those obtainable within the U.S.; and (2) many American corporations and individual businessmen found highly profitable manufacturing opportunities abroad.[2] This, however, only tells one side of the foreign-investment story— the "outward" foreign investment.

Foreign investment in the U.S., often being termed "inward investment" and "reverse investment" by some authors, did not draw American people's attention until the early 1970's. One government source reported:

> . . . Before the 1970's the volume of foreign investment in the United States was limited by a variety of factors, not the least of which was the inability of foreign firms to compete in the U.S. market. After 1970, however, the climate for foreign investors and foreign firms improved and the flow of investments in the United States increased dramatically.[3]

The increased U.S. domestic concern over inward investment in the recent years can be explained by the following reasons: (1) the awareness of the suddenly accelerated growth in the volume of inward investment; (2) the fear of economic takeovers by the newly-rich OPEC (Oil Production and Export Cartel) nations; and (3) simple xenophobia.[4]

Noticing the recent surge of foreign investment in the U.S., the Congress passed a Foreign Investment Study Act in 1974, which was later signed by the President into Public Law 93-479. Under this act, the U.S. Department of Commerce completed a benchmark survey of foreign direct investment and published the results in April 1976. The nature, scope, magnitude, motives and various effects of such investment activities were the major topics investigated.[5]

Foreign investment in the U.S. can be divided into two classes: (1) foreign direct investment, which is defined in terms of foreign ownership of 10 percent or more of the voting interest in a business enterprise incorporated in the U.S., or an equivalent interest in an unincorporated business enterprise; and (2) foreign portfolio investment, which refers to foreign purchases of U.S. government bonds, bonds and stocks of American corporations, and some other valuable commercial certificates.[6]

The foreign direct investment can be further broken down by industry as shown in Figure 2-1. This study investigated the plant location decisions of foreign manufacturing investors in the U.S. Neither the foreign portfolio investment nor the "finance, insurance and real estate," "wholesale trade," "petroleum," and "other" sectors in the foreign direct investment were concerns in this study.

Before considering the choice of a plant location, the foreign manufacturing investors were normally faced with a more basic decision of whether or not to manufacture in the U.S. at all. It is important, therefore, to examine the foreign manufacturing investors' motives to come to the U.S.

Since the interest in foreign manufacturing investment in the U.S. was developed after 1970, most literature on the subject of motivation of foreign manufacturing investment concerns American outward investment, rather than inward investment from foreign countries.[7] As an example, Gunnar Beeth, an experienced international operating manager and management consultant, summarized the main reasons why American manufacturing investors venture into overseas business as follows:

> (1) To harvest the profits—with your company's know-how, you can harvest the profits not only from your domestic market, but also from the whole world; (2) to be close to new technical developments and trends in customer desires—because many new technical developments originate in Europe and Japan, your being on the scene, in close contact with your customers, will enable you to send back and exploit these new ideas much sooner than a purely domestic company can; (3) to avoid giving foreign competitors the edge—suppose your company has a strong position only in the United States and leaves the remainder of the world market uncovered. That gives a foreign competitor the opportunity to grow so strong abroad in the vacuum. you have left him that he may later open up shop in the United States and challenge you; (4) to utilize lower labor costs in manufacturing; (5) to get manufacturing inside certain customs duty or import license barriers or into a preferred country of origin or a low tax area, or to meet local, chauvinistic safety requirements; (6) to locate near the sources of supply; (7) to get away from trust-busters at home who don't allow you expansion there.[8]

FIGURE 2-1.
FOREIGN DIRECT INVESTMENT IN THE U.S. BY INDUSTRY

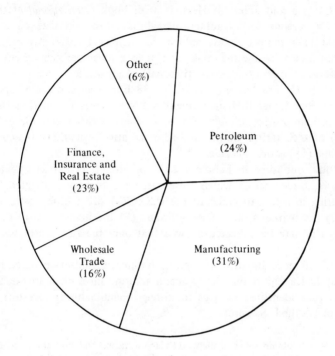

Source: U.S. Department of Commerce, *Foreign Direct Investment in the United States* (Washington, D.C.: U.S. Government Printing Office, 1976), Vol. 1, p. 21.

Although it is wrong to apply the reasoning for American firms directly to foreign manufacturing investors in the U.S., there should be values in reviewing the corresponding situation.

Discussing alternative strategies of entering foreign markets, Professors Philip R. Cateora and John M. Hess, in their book *International Marketing,* presented six reasons for manufacturing abroad: "to capitalize on low-cost labor, avoid high import taxes, reduce the high costs of transportation to market, gain access to raw materials, and/or as a means of gaining entry into other markets . . . to gain the 'production-sharing' advantage."[9]

Lawrence G. Franko, in a survey of 38 European companies operating in the U.S., found that their investment motives were: "(1) market size and affluence; (2) innovative stimuli of U.S. business environment; (3) existence (or threat) of U.S. tariffs, quotas and administrative regulations; (4) customer pressures; and (5) historical accident."[10]

A study, published in February 1973 by Robert B. Leftwich, examined the following three factors which were suspected to have motivated foreign manufacturing investors to come to the U.S.: "(1) size of the host country's market; (2) the market's rate of growth; and (3) the home country's level of tariffs."[11] The data he collected showed that only the first factor was significant.

The Conference Board, a non-profit business organization based in New York, published a report on foreign manufacturing investment in the U.S. in 1974. The four identified motives for foreign manufacturing investors to set up operations in the U.S. were:

> . . . to obtain a slice of the world's largest, richest and most competitive market . . . to learn from the experience of its U.S. affiliates in the fields of management, marketing, product planning, research, etc., for the benefit of its home operations . . . (to gain) the advantage of exporting from the U.S. to third markets . . . (to get access to) the U.S. capital market, which offers a wide variety of instruments and maturities to the would-be borrower.[12]

While most relevant studies indicated that foreign manufacturing investors came to the U.S. because certain problems could be solved or some advantages could be gained in the U.S., the Arthur D. Little Company, in a study prepared for the U.S. Department of Commerce, specifically emphasized the changes which occurred within foreign companies and foreign nations in recent years. It was concluded that:

> . . . the growth in the size and the capacity of foreign based corporations has provided the foreign firms with the expertise necessary to make viable overseas investments . . . there is the ability of foreign nations to support outward investments. Before 1970 the economics of many nations simply could not afford large capital outflows.[13]

In a report prepared by the staff of the Committee on Banking, Currency and Housing, House of Representatives, the continued growth of foreign investment in the U.S. was explained by the following factors:

> . . . (1) size and opportunities of the U.S. market; (2) the ability of the U.S. to be one of the first nations to overcome the world-wide recession of 1973-1974; (3) the steady growth of the Eurodollar market which has provided the liquidity necessary for expanded investments; (4) political uncertainties in other countries, such as the rise of Communism in Italy and nationalistic developments in England; (5) the role of labor unions in the U.S. as compared to those of Western Europe; (6) the desire of many foreign firms to gain experience from investments in the United States; and finally (7) the presence of U.S. governmental restrictions on imports which serve to protect the foreign firms once they are established within this country.[14]

Tom Foster, the associate editor of *Distribution Worldwide,* listed the following reasons as the major determinants of the recent wave of reverse investment: "(1) establishment or expansion of marketing opportunities that were unavailable or unfeasible in the home country; (2) eroding profits in the domestic operation caused by uncontrollable cost factors such as wage hikes, government regulations and inflation; (3) availability of raw materials, labor, capital, technology and space that was unavailable in the home country; (4) favorable monetary exchange rates because of recent devaluations of the dollar; (5) political stability in the U.S."[15]

In an interview study including 40 foreign firms, John D. Daniels presented a rather lengthy and detailed analysis about why they decided to enter the U.S. production. The nine factors discussed were:

> . . . (1) it has become more difficult for many foreign producers to continue to increase sales and profits in the home market; (2) such industries as aviation, electronics, certain scientific instruments, and certain metal alloys have shifted to and become more concentrated in the U.S.; (3) consumers in the U.S. are in many instances leading indicators of what will be accepted abroad at a later time; (4) foreign lags in product development and acceptance are decreasing; (5) the growing antitrust action against large firms (in the U.S.) made it easier for them to come into the U.S.; (6) the U.S. government policies restricted their ability to export to the American market; (7) American industries have exerted pressures on foreign firms through their own "buy American" policies; (8) different products are needed for the U.S. market; and (9) certain products almost have to be produced locally to be competitive.[16]

A SURVEY OF LOCATION THEORY

The subject of location has been studied by two different groups of scholars. Geographers have emphasized the spatial patterns of location through case studies, while economists have had primary interest in optimum allocation of resources by means of theoretical reasoning.[17] The major purpose of this section is to describe and justify the plant location factors that are considered important by leading theoreticians. Since this study's concern is only with plant location decisions rather than with the entire field of spatial economics and economic geography, the literature discussing topics like agricultural land use, distribution of towns and cities, and location of retail stores is either completely omitted or just briefly touched.

George Renner

Among the early economic geographers, Renner was the first person who stated his ideas concerning industrial location as general principles. The six component elements identified were raw materials, market, labor (including management), power, capital, and transportation. His principle of industrial location reads as follows:

> An industry tends to locate at a point which provides optimum access to its ingredients or component elements. If all these component elements are juxtaposed, the location of the industry is predetermined. If, however, they occur widely separated, the industry is so located as to be most accessible to that element which would be the most expensive or difficult to transport and which, therefore, becomes the locative factor for the industry in question.[18]

He classified industries into four categories: extractive, reproductive, fabricative, and facilitative. Although his principle is general in nature, its application is different with each of the four categories of industries. About the fabricative (or manufacturing) industry, which is this study's major concern, Renner said:

> Any manufactural industry tends to locate at a point which provides optimum access to its ingredient elements. It will, therefore, seek a site near to: (a) Raw Material, if it uses perishable or highly condensible raw substances or (b) Market, where the processing adds fragility, perishability, weight, or bulk to the raw materials, or where its products are subject to rapid changes in style, design, or technological character or (c) Power, where the mechanical energy costs of processing are the chief item in the total cost or (d) Labor, where its wages to skilled artisans are a large item in the total cost.[19]

Renner used such terms and concepts as disjunctive symbiosis, conjunctive symbiosis, and coindustrialization to discuss externalities and agglomeration tendencies. His main contributions lay in his bringing together many location factors and making geographers more aware of the relevant works of economists.[20]

E. L. Ullman and M. F. Dacey

According to economic-base theory, industries in a city can be divided into two types. The nonbasic industries are those that produce for the consumption of the city itself, while those that produce for outside markets are termed basic industries. In an investigation of the relationship between industrial structure and city size, Ullman and Dacey developed a minimum requirement approach, which proposes that: "(1) there is a minimum requirement for every industry to satisfy local demand; and (2) the nonbasic employment tends to increase with the size of the city."[21] City size was herein used as a surrogate for market size. It was maintained that, for an economic base, analyses of its industrial structure and market structure would be useful in predicting new industrial development and explaining industrial location.

E. M. Rawstron

In the late 1950's, Rawstron offered three principles of industrial location: principle of physical restriction, principle of economic restriction, and principle of technical restriction. The principle of physical restriction is related to the production of natural resources. In the principle of economic restriction, the five cost factors are labor, materials, land, marketing, and capital. Cost on each factor varies from location to location. This principle "embodies the concept of spatial margins to profitability where costs become too great for industries to be economically viable."[22] The principle of technical restriction addresses the relationship between the level of technology and industrial location; Rawstron's idea was that "if an industrialist knows that his plant will need frequent modification to keep up with technical progress he may not pay great attention to his location, but as technical improvements become less frequent, locational economies may become more important."[23]

Allen Pred

In recent years, geographers have noted that past discussions about industrial location tended to have a bias toward economic determinism.[24] In reality, the world is populated by people with imperfect knowledge, with limited ability to use information, and in pursuit of both material and nonmaterial ends. Pred followed this kind of thinking and explained the locational decision by a "behavioral matrix," shown as Figure 2-2. He explained:

> A position toward the bottom right of the matrix indicates a good level of knowledge as well as good ability to use it, and there would be a high degree of probability of a good choice of location, perhaps one near the economic optimum. As knowledge and ability decrease, toward the top left of the matrix, the probability of good locational choice is reduced. The emphasis is on probability because good knowledge and ability are not a guarantee of a good choice of location (though they make it very likely), just as there is an outside chance that a firm with little knowledge of the alternatives and a poor management could be lucky enough to make a good decision.[25]

FIGURE 2-2.
THE BEHAVIORAL MATRIX

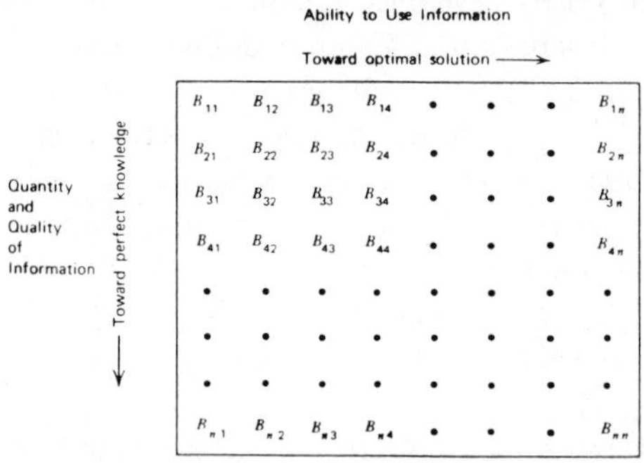
Ability to Use Information
Toward optimal solution
Quantity and Quality of Information
Toward perfect knowledge

Source: *Behavior and Location: Foundations for a Geographic and Dynamic Location Theory,* Part I, cited by David M. Smith, *Industrial Location* (New York: John Wiley & Sons, Inc., 1971), p. 106.

Johann Henrich Von Thünen

Recognized as the first person who systematically analyzed and explained the location of economic activity, Von Thünen published his book *Der Isolierte Staat in Beziehung auf Landwirtschaft und Nationalokonomie* in 1826.[26] As an agriculturalist, he addressed himself to the problem of where agricultural production of various crops would take place within a given homogeneous territory. Since material deposit and labor were assumed to be evenly distributed throughout the territory, transport expense and the price of land were the two major costs being discussed. His general conclusions included: (1) "those commodities that can not readily absorb transport expense will be located (or produced) near the market and vice versa;"[27] and (2) "as distance from the market increases, intensive cultivation is replaced by extensive cultivation."[28]

Alfred Weber

It is generally agreed by leading writers that the development of modern industrial location theory began with Weber's book, entitled *Uber den Standort der Industrien,* published in 1909.[29] While Von Thünen's concern was agriculture-oriented, Weber's interest was in the locational problems of industrial firms. The way he classified location factors was:

1. General regional factors
   a. Transportation factors
   b. Labor factors
2. General local factors
   a. Agglomerating factors
   b. Deglomerating factors
3. Natural factors
4. Social factors[30]

One thing which should be noted is that although Weber mentioned "natural factors" and "social factors" in his classification of location factors, he actually did not use them in his analysis. One major conclusion he reached reads:

The precise point at which an industry locates may be at (1) the point of consumption in weight-gaining processes, (2) the point of production in weight-losing processes, or (3) some point in between where the weight gain or weight loss is equal or not important in a particular case.[31]

August Lösch

The unrealistic assumption about market demand and the sales potential virtually being ignored were the two criticisms against the early location theories. In 1940, Lösch used demand as the major variable in the development of a general location theory. He argued that neither "least cost" nor "maximum revenue" should determine an industrial firm's location. He said, "The right approach is to find the place of maximum profits, where total revenue exceeds total cost by the greatest amount."[32]

In his book *The Economics of Location,* Lösch recognized the following factors as influential to location decisions:

1. Transport costs
2. Time costs
3. Selling costs
4. Business risks
5. "Idiosyncrasies"—climate, habit, income
6. Extent of business—plant expansion
7. Hindrances to trade
8. Entrepreneurial and managerial disinclination and incompetence
9. Factor accessibility
10. Factor productivity
11. Tariffs
12. Human differences
13. Differences in politics
14. Reactions of other firms[33]

Edgar Hoover

In 1937, Hoover published his *Location Theory and the Shoe and Leather Industries,*[34] containing both theories and case studies. About ten years later, he wrote another book, *The Location of Economic Activity.*[35] Building on the work of Von Thünen and Weber, Hoover included both demand and institutional factors in his analysis. He noted that in the real world the transport facilities were nonuniformly distributed and the freight rates were affected by institutional forces. This led him to conclude that freight rate did not increase proportionately with distance. Therefore, he criticized the simple homogeneous model of space economy and emphasized the nonlinear nature of freight rates in his study.

Hoover classified cost factors into:

1.   *Transportation costs* of
    a. procuring raw materials, and
    b. distributing the finished product
2.   *Production costs* which depend on
    a. factor prices, and
    b. quantities of factors needed for production[36]

He further divided the "production costs" into six items: "(1) direct labor costs; (2) administration costs; (3) interest; (4) rent and royalties; (5) maintenance and depreciation; and (6) taxes."[37]

In regard to natural factors, he commented:

> Soil, climate, and topography are important direct determinants of yield in agriculture and forestry and affect the efficiency of almost any process. A hot climate, for instance, is likely to curtail output per man hour in manufacturing or trade and thus to raise unit labor costs—though the employer may prefer to shift the extra cost to other items such as interest and electric power by installing air conditioning. Cold climates necessitate heavier and more costly construction. Construction and maintenance costs may also be higher when soil and topographic features are unfavorable.[38]

Melvin L. Greenhut

Greenhut's two books, *Plant Location in Theory and in Practice* (1956) and *Microeconomics and Space Economy* (1963), together with his many published papers, made him a giant in the field of spatial economics. Challenging the earlier theorists' assumptions such as a given price and constant demand, he maintained that demand should be considered as a major location variable.[39] In his perception, the demand factor is divisible into six items:

1.   The shape of the demand curve for a given product.
2.   The location of competitors, which in turn partially determines
    a. the magnitude of the demand, and
    b. the cross-elasticity of demand at different places
3.   The significance of proximity, type of service, and speed of service; prejudices of consumers
4.   The relationship between personal contacts and sales
5.   The extent of the market area, which itself is partially determined by cost factors and pricing policies
6.   The competitiveness of the industry in location and price; certainty and uncertainty.[40]

Greenhut followed in the footsteps of his predecessors in the sense that he kept cost as an important factor to plant location decisions. He separated the cost elements into several groups:

1.   The cost of land, which includes
    a. the rent of land;

      b. the tax on land;
      c. the availability of capital, which partially depends upon
         (1) the banking facilities and financial resources, and
         (2) personal contacts;
      d. the cost of capital, which is also partially dependent upon
         (1) the banking facilities and financial resources and
         (2) the type of climate;
      e. the insurance rates at different sites, which in turn partially depend upon
         (1) the banking facilities and financial resources,
         (2) the police and fire protection, and
         (3) the type of climate;
      f. the cost of fuel and power, which is partially dependent upon
         (1) natural resources,
         (2) topography, and
         (3) climate.
2.   The cost of labor and management, which is influenced by
      a. the health of the community, the park and education facilities, housing facilities, wage differences, etc., and
      b. state laws.
3.   The cost of materials and equipment which is partially determined by
      a. the location of competitors (sellers and buyers),
      b. the price system in the supply area (f.o.b. mill, equalizing or other forms of discriminatory delivered prices),
      c. the extent of the supply area, which in turn is partially dependent upon
         (1) personal contacts and
         (2) price policy.
4.   The cost of transportation, which is partially determined by
      a. the topography
      b. the transport facilities and
      c. the characteristics of the product.[41]

Greenhut is known for being the first theorist to include personal factors into the consideration of plant location decisions. According to his classification, the purely personal factors include:

1.   The importance of psychic income (size of plant),
2.   Environmental preferences, and
3.   The security motive.[42]

In his discussion of location factors, Greenhut indicated that there were many different ways of classifying them and a factor could rightfully appear in more than one category.[43] In one chapter of his book, *Plant Location in Theory and in Practice,* he contrasted general location factors to specific location factors and said, "General (location) factors are state or regional forces . . . specific (location) factors direct the location to a particular city or district within a city."[44] In another chapter of the same book, he grouped location factors into seven categories: "(1) cost factors; (2) demand factors; (3) cost-reducing factors; (4) revenue-increasing factors; (5) personal cost-reducing factors; (6) personal revenue-increasing factors; and (7) purely personal considerations."[45]

Walter Isard

A recognized pioneering contributor to the evolving discipline of regional science, Isard wrote two important books on location theory: *Location and Space Economy* (1956) and *Methods of Regional Analysis* (1960).[46] Regional science has its focus on three interrelated topics: (1) location; (2) scale of operations; and (3) flow.[47] Isard did not add much, if any, to the existing location-factor list, but he classified these factors differently from other writers. His classification was:

1. Transport costs and certain other transfer costs.
2. The costs associated with labor, power, water, taxes, insurance, interest (as payment for the services of capital), climate, topography, social and political milieu, and a number of other items.
3. The diverse elements which give rise to agglomeration and deglomeration economies.
    a. agglomeration economies:
        (1) economies of scale (internal to firm),
        (2) localization economies (external to firm),
        (3) urbanization economies (external to firm).
    b. deglomeration economies:
        (1) internal diseconomies to size,
        (2) increased rents and service costs due to population density and congestion,
        (3) increased costs of living, particularly food costs.[48]

A significant contribution that Isard made was his striving to fuse the location theory with the so-called "substitution principle." George M. McManmon presented an excellent summary of Isard's substitution approach to location decision:

> He (Isard) holds that the proper location decision requires discovery of the transport optimal point, at which point the correct substitution prevails between pairs of transport inputs. After he establishes his basic concepts and applies the substitution principle to transport inputs, he then considers other kinds of orientation, such as labor, power, rents, and various other costs substitutable for transport outlays. His substitution principle moves beyond the matter of costs to the matter of demand and embraces such factors as shifting locations and changes in market area divisions.[49]

A SURVEY OF RELATED EMPIRICAL STUDIES

A search for related empirical literature found only two previous studies which, to a certain extent, have dealt with the problems investigated in the present study. In both of them, however, the plant location decision was just treated as a sub-topic and the sample sizes were rather small. The point is that neither of them can be adequately called an in-depth location study. A third study which is reviewed in this section is one focusing on American and European multinational firms.

John D. Daniels

In 1971, Daniels studied some basic aspects of foreign manufacturing investment in the U.S., including such items as events preceding the U.S. investment, investment policies, methods and motives for entering U.S. production, and evaluations of the U.S. investment experience. Data were obtained from 40 foreign firms which had their first U.S. manufacturing investments after 1954.

Daniels found that a little less than 50 percent of his respondent firms actually did not make any plant location decision. This was because they either accepted the locations of existing firms when a "buy-in" approach was used or let the U.S. partners make the decision in the case of a joint venture. For those buy-in cases, "the U.S. facility usually had some asset the foreign firm felt that it did not have in sufficient quantity to transfer to a new operation; the most common of these were management and technical personnel . . ."[50] Table 2-1 presents Daniels' findings in this regard:

TABLE 2-1
MAJOR IMPETUS FOR CHOOSING A REGION FOR A
MANUFACTURING INVESTMENT IN THE
UNITED STATES

Major Impetus	Number of Firms
No decision by investors:	
Accepted location of existing firm when "buy-in" took place	16
U.S. partner made the decision	2
Decision made by investors:	
Nearness to home operation	9
Nearness to operations in a "third country"	2
Nearness to inexpensive or abundant production factors	4
Nearness to market	7
Total	40

Source: John D. Daniels, *Recent Foreign Direct Manufacturing Investment in the United States* (New York: Praeger Publishers, Inc., 1971), p. 65.

Daniels pointed out that there were three levels of decisions concerning plant location: a general area, a specific community, and a particular site.[51] Based on his factual finding, he made the following comment:

> One should expect foreign firms to be governed in their location choice by the same factors that affect the location of industry by domestic firms. Cost, market, and non-economic factors are considered both by the foreign investors and domestic investors; however, there are conditions that differentiate the results of the consideration . . . what might be an optimum cost location for a domestic firm may not be so for the foreign firm coming into

the United States. The difference is due to an integration of activites between the U.S. and home operations. The maximization of corporate profits may not necessarily maximize the U.S. profits.[52]

Jeffrey S. Arpan and David A. Ricks

In a research study including 100 foreign manufacturers, Arpan and Ricks found that the vast majority (86 percent) of them initiated U.S. operations by building entirely new companies, rather than buying into existing ones.[53] This conclusion conflicts with Daniels' finding. With regard to factors affecting which state and community to invest in, the results are shown in Table 2-2. The sources from which these 100 foreign manufacturing investors collected their informtion to make plant location decisions in the U.S. are summarized in Table 2-3.

TABLE 2-2
FACTORS AFFECTING FOREIGN MANUFACTURERS REGARDING THEIR LOCATING PLANTS IN A PARTICULAR STATE OR COMMUNITY [a]

	Percent of Respondents	
	State	Community
Proximity to markets	34%	25%
Transportation facilities	24	NA [b]
Labor factors	15	23
Tax considerations	9	11

[a] Adapted from Jeffrey S. Arpan and David A. Ricks, *Directory of Foreign Manufacturers in the United States* (Atlanta: School of Business Administration, Georgia State University, 1975), p. xv.

[b] Not available.

Hans Schollhammer

While most location studies were done within the boundary of a single country, Schollhammer did a survey collecting data from 140 multinational corporations (95 U.S. firms, 45 European firms).[54] His study was not limited by the boundary of any specific country. The question he asked can be paraphrased as: what was the importance of each of the relevant factors regarding in which country to locate the international investor's manufacturing plant? He classified 78 location factors into eight categories. The five most important and the five least important country-related location factors were identified (See Table 2-4 and Table 2-5).

TABLE 2-3

COMMUNICATION SOURCES USED BY FOREIGN MANUFACTURING
INVESTORS TO MAKE THEIR PLANT LOCATION DECISIONS [a]

Information Sources	State	Community
Other firms	34% [b]	28%
Investment missions	19	19
State agencies	14	18
U.S. Dept. of Commerce	14	13
Other sources	19	22

[a] Adapted from Jeffrey S. Arpan and David A. Ricks, *Directory of Foreign Manufacturers in the United States* (Atlanta, Georgia: School of Business Administration, Georgia State University, 1975), p. xv.

[b] Percent of the respondents.

OTHER RELATED LITERATURE

Professor Donald J. Bowersox, in his book *Logistical Management,*[55] developed a plant location procedure, which nicely puts the various location factors into a working framework. This suggested procedure consists of two steps: plant analysis and field analysis. The purpose of plant analysis is to develop a set of relevant location specifications, which serves as a starting point and foundation for the field analysis. Location alternatives need to be evaluated at three levels: regional, community, and site. The reduction process from general areas to specific locations was referred to as field analysis. Bowersox said, ". . . field analysis procedure is not viewed as a limiting process; selection of the one best community need not be made prior to conducting a search for satisfactory factory sites."[56]

Being an industrial practitioner with experience in both plant engineering and production planning, Ronald H. Hermone developed his version of location procedure, which, as a matter of fact, is very similar to Bowersox's, but he discussed in more detail the specific information needed at each decision stage, and where and how to get various kinds of useful information.[57] He believes that the subjective factors, including housing, education, health care, recreation, and cultural activities, are more important in the selection of communities and plant sites than in the selection of regions.[58]

Charging that location surveys often mislead eager-to-grow communities to make costly but misdirected efforts, T.E. McMillan, Jr. pointed out that "the 'why' a plant official chose a region may be vastly different from what determined his selection of a particular site or community."[59] Charles Russell Beaton, Jr. appeared to hold the same kind of opinion when he stated, ". . . the location decision may be segmented into several separate location decisions, each involving distinctly different locational variables, according to geographic range of variation or level of constancy; it is a mistake to analyze the effect of all variables simultaneously, since they are never considered together."[60]

TABLE 2-4
TOP FIVE PLANT LOCATION FACTORS FOR MULTINATIONAL FIRMS, BY NATIONAL ORIGIN [a]

Ranking	United States	England	France	West Germany
1	Size of market for your product(s)	Size of market for your product(s)	Size of market for your product(s)	Presence of nationalization threat
2	Rate of growth of this market	Rate of growth of this market	Rate of growth of this market	Existence of laws for the protection of property rights
3	Remittance of profits regulations	Remittance of profits regulations	Presence of nationalization threat	Government's attitude toward foreign investment
4	Government's attitude toward foreign investment	Government's attitude toward foreign investment	Government's attitude toward foreign investment	Personal safety of aliens and their personal property
5	Convertibility of currency	Tax rates (corporate, turnover, local taxes, etc.)	Existence of clear corporate investment laws	Availability of suitable plant sites

[a] Adapted from Hans Schollhammer, *Locational Strategies of Multinational Firms* (Los Angeles: Center for International Business, Pepperdine University, 1974), p. 20.

In order to ease the work of identifying all the important plant location factors, some authors have provided a "checklist of site selection" and the like. The most complete list of this kind was developed by the editors of *Site Selection Handbook.*[61] Two similar but less extensive lists can be found in *Distribution Worldwide* and *Physical Distribution Management.*[62]

Plant Location and *Site Selection Handbook* are two highly useful magazines to plant locators.[63] *Plant Location,* an annual publication covering both U.S. and Canada, presents such data as population, labor, raw materials, transportation, utilities, climate, tax information, and people to contact at both state (or province) and city (25,000 or more) levels. *Site Selection Handbook* is also published annually. While *Plant Location* offers data state by state and city by city, *Site Selection Handbook* presents data factor by factor. This certainly makes comparison work easier.

TABLE 2-5

BOTTOM FIVE PLANT LOCATION FACTORS FOR MULTINATIONAL
FIRMS, BY NATIONAL ORIGIN [a]

Ranking	United States	England	France	West Germany
74	Availability of U.S. Government investment insurance	Availability and cost of export financing	Antitrust vulnerability	State of marketing and distribution system
75	Proximity to export markets	Availability of local agencies for market research and promotional activities	Rate of population growth	Rate of population growth
76	Availability and cost of export financing	Attitude of local competitors toward foreign investments	Worker productivity	Proximity to export markets
77	Existence of a national economic plan	Availability of British Government investment insurance	Availability of local agencies for market research and promotional activities	Existence of a national economic plan
78	Availability of local agencies for market research and promotional activities	Treaty of friendship, commerce and navigation with the home country	Availability of English speaking managerial, technical, office personnel	Availability of local agencies for market research and promotional activities

[a] Adapted from Hans Schollhammer, *Locational Strategies of Multinational Firms* (Los Angeles: Center for International Business, Pepperdine University, 1974), p. 22.

SUMMARY

Concerns with economic development have been instrumental in arousing the United States' interest in inward foreign manufacturing investment, which can effectively increase the employment level, balance international transactions, reduce inflationary pressures, and raise production efficiency. Since the reasons foreigners invest in the U.S. have a decided effect on where they will locate their plants, this chapter begins with an examination of foreign manufacturing investors' motives coming to the U.S. Next, location theories developed by leading geographers and economists are reviewed to identify the plant location factors which might have influenced foreign manufacturing investors in the U.S. Third, three related empirical studies are discussed. No in-depth plant location study of foreign manufacturing investment in the U.S. was found. Finally, some other related literature which has not been included in the discussion of the early three sections is presented.

The plant location factors of primary importance to foreign manufacturing investors in the U.S., as indicated and implied from this chapter's review and discussion, are listed below:

1. Nearness to markets within the U.S.
2. Proximity to export markets (outside the U.S.)
3. Nearness to home operation
4. Nearness to operations in a "third country"
5. Facilities of import and export
6. Proximity to raw material sources
7. Proximity to suppliers
8. Availability of managerial and technical personnel
9. Availability of skilled labor
10. Availability of unskilled labor
11. Salary and wage rate
12. Labor attitudes
13. Labor laws
14. Availability of utilities
15. Cost of utilities
16. Availability of transportation facilities
17. Cost of transportation facilities
18. Availability of suitable plant sites
19. Cost of suitable land
20. Cost of construction
21. Ample space for future expansion
22. Availability of local capital fund
23. Cost of local capital fund
24. State tax rates
25. Local tax rates
26. Government incentives
27. Attitudes of government officials
28. Attitudes of local citizens
29. Housing facilities
30. Education facilities
31. Police and fire protection
32. Climate

CHAPTER III

METHODOLOGY

INTRODUCTION

With respect to the problems raised and the hypotheses formulated in Chapter I, no adequate empirical data were found in a thorough review of previous studies. This meant that primary data had to be gathered for the project at hand.

Primary data are generally gathered by one of the following three methods: observation, experimentation, and survey. A survey can be done in person, by telephone, or by mail. In this study, the mail survey method was chosen based on the nature of the information sought, the width of geographical area covered, and the availability of time, money, personnel, and facilities. A mail survey, like any other data-collection methods, has its advantages and disadvantages. Efforts were made to keep these disadvantages at their lowest possible levels. The detailed research design and plan are presented in the following order: (1) population and frame; (2) design of the questionnaire; (3) data collection and processing; and (4) analysis of data. Returns of the pretest and the full-scale study are also reported in this chapter.

POPULATION AND FRAME

The population was composed of all the foreign manufacturing investors in the U.S. that met the following criteria:

1. The company produces physical products.
2. It is in "manufacturing" industries; the population excludes foreign manufacturers who are in "metals mining" or "coal mining" or "non-metallic mining" or "oil and gas extraction" industries, but includes those who manufacture "petroleum and related products."[1]
3. A plant in the U.S. is required as evidence that a plant location decision was made sometimes in the past.
4. Ten percent or more of the company's ownership belongs to non-Americans.[2]

The frame of the population was formed from three sources: (1) the *Directory of Foreign Manufacturers in the United States,* which was compiled by Professors Jeffrey S. Arpan and David A. Ricks in the spring of 1975 and later updated in June, 1976;[3] (2) the *Foreign Direct Investors in the United States,* which was published by the U.S. Department of Commerce in March, 1976;[4] and (3) lists of foreign manufacturers provided by states' economic development agencies.[5] According to this frame, the population size of this study was 1147. Distributions of foreign manufacturing plants over national origin, standard industrial classification (SIC) code and state of plant location are presented in Tables 3-1, 3-2, and 3-3. A foreign manufacturer, according to the definition adopted in this research, may have more than one plant.

DESIGN OF THE QUESTIONNAIRE

The questionnaire consisted of two sections.[6] Section I was designed to gain certain identification and classification information of foreign manufacturing investors, such as time of the plant location decision made, categories of major products produced, number of employees, state of plant location, percentage of foreign ownership, national origin of the principal non-American investors, and information sources used. Section II contained a list of 32 plant location factors. The respondents were asked to indicate how important each of these plant location factors was when they chose a particular community in which to locate their plant. A standard five-point scale ranging from "not at all important" to "extremely important" was used. To make the questionnaire easy to read and answer, boldfaced characters were used at the places where considered appropriate and most questions only required placing check marks in the spaces provided.

TABLE 3-1
THE DISTRIBUTION OF FOREIGN MANUFACTURING PLANTS
OVER NATIONAL ORIGIN [a]

Country	Number	Percent
Canada	457	22.6
France	170	8.3
Germany	282	13.7
Japan	199	9.7 [b]
Netherlands	158	7.7
Sweden	47	2.3
Switzerland	150	7.3
United Kingdom	358	17.4
Other	232	11.0
Total	2,053	100.0

[a] Adapted from U.S. Department of Commerce, *Foreign Direct Investment in the United States* (Washington, D.C.: U.S. Government Printing Office, 1976), 3:A-126.

[b] "May be understated, since no official data were obtainable for California, where Japanese investors are particularly active."—a direct quote from the above source.

TABLE 3-2
THE DISTRIBUTION OF FOREIGN MANUFACTURING PLANTS
OVER SIC CODE [a]

SIC Code	Number	Percent
20	217	10.6
22	90	4.4
26	50	2.4
28	336	16.4
30	96	4.7
32	53	2.6
33	49	2.4
34	327	15.9
35	184	9.0
36	180	8.8
38	66	2.9
Other	405	19.9
Total	2,053	100.0

[a] Adapted from U.S. Department of Commerce, *Foreign Direct Investment in the United States* (Washington, D.C.: U.S. Government Printing Office, 1976), 3:A-127.

DATA COLLECTION

In addition to paying special attention toward the preparation of the questionnaire, the following six steps were done to increase the return rate of this mail survey:

1. A cover letter from the Dean of the College of Business Administration at the University of Nebraska-Lincoln was used to introduce the researcher to the respondents and to solicit their cooperation.[7]

2. A second cover letter from the researcher was used to explain to the respondents what this study was all about and why it was in their best interests to reply.[8]

3. A summary report of this study was promised to the respondents free of charge as soon as it was available.

4. It was made clear that all the returned questionnaires would be treated confidentially. The findings would be reported in the form of statistical summaries, with the identification of any individual firm made impossible.

5. A business reply envelope was mailed to the respondent along with the cover letters and the questionnaire. The return address used was the Bureau of Business Research of the University of Nebraska-Lincoln.

6. A follow-up letter was sent to the respondents three weeks after the questionnaires were mailed. Since it was difficult to identify which firms had responded and which firms had not, most of the firms on the first mailing list were sent the follow-up letter.[9]

TABLE 3-3
THE DISTRIBUTION OF FOREIGN MANUFACTURING PLANTS
OVER STATE OF PLANT LOCATION [a]

State	Number	Percent
Georgia	68	3.3
Illinois	92	4.5
Indiana	47	2.3
Massachusetts	74	3.6
New Jersey	178	8.7
New York	222	10.8
North Carolina	90	4.4
Ohio	51	2.5
Pennsylvania	125	6.1
South Carolina	71	3.5
Texas	82	4.0
Virginia	58	2.8
Other	895	43.5
Total	2,053	100.0

[a] Adapted from. U.S. Department of Commerce, *Foreign Direct Investment in the United States* (Washington, D.C.: U.S. Government Printing Office, 1976), 3:A-123-A-125.

PRETEST

The questionnaire was pre-tested on a random sample of 50 foreign manufacturing investors. This pretesting served two functions: (1) to improve the construction of the questionnaire: biased questions were eliminated, ambiguous questions clarified, and those exceeding respondents' ability and willingness to answer modified; and (2) to ascertain response rate.

The response to the pretest is summarized in Figure 3-1. Thirty-four percent of the questionnaires mailed were returned, and 24 percent were usable. Those returns classified as "unusable" were due to one of the following four reasons: (1) the company was no longer in existence; (2) it was no longer a foreign company; (3) it was not a foreign company in the first place; and (4) it had less than ten percent foreign ownership.

Since the follow-up letters generated seven responses, which accounted for 41 percent of the total returns, it was decided that they should be used again in the full-scale study.

THE FULL-SCALE STUDY

On September 1, 1977, questionnaires and cover letters were mailed to 1,097 foreign manufacturers in the U.S. which were not previously included in the prestest. The response to the full-scale study was shown in Figure 3-2.

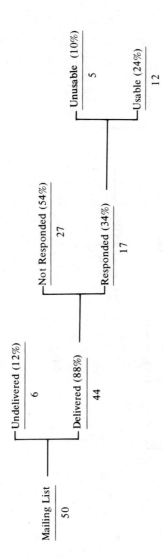

FIGURE 3-1 RESPONSE TO THE PRETEST

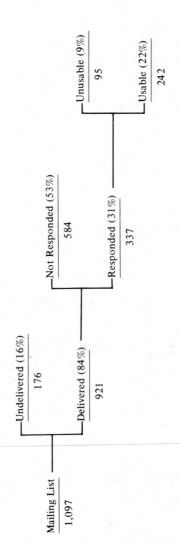

FIGURE 3-2 RESULT OF THE FULL-SCALE STUDY

The response rate was 31 percent. Of the 337 returns, 242, or 22 percent, provided usable information. This outcome was a definite improvement compared to the two related previous empirical studies; Daniels obtained his data from 40 foreign firms and Arpan and Ricks' study included 100 foreign manufacturers.[10]

There was a total of 95 unusable returns. Forty-two respondents said that they were just foreign distributors and do no manufacturing in the U.S. Twenty-eight firms claimed to be wholly American-owned. Another 13 filled out the questionnaire, but indicated that the foreign ownership was zero per cent. Six replied, "Do not apply." Reasons such as "no longer in existence," "due to the company's policy, do not fill out the questionnaire," "too much time is required to answer," "prefer not to answer the questionnaire," and "can not recall because the plant location decision was made long time ago" accounted for the rest of the unusables.

The usable returns from the pretest and the full-scale study were combined for analysis, giving a total of 254 responses out of 1,147 total requests, or 22 percent. It was considered acceptable to combine the pretest and the full-scale-study returns because: (1) the questions asked were the same (only two printing corrections were made); (2) the time elapsed between mailings was only five weeks. Since plant location decisions tend to be made on a long term basis, five weeks should not affect the results in any significant ways.

ANALYSIS OF DATA

General characteristics of the responding foreign manufacturing investors

Based on the returned usable questionnaires, five tables were constructed to provide detailed information regarding the characteristics of the responding firms which had made plant location decisions in the U.S. These tables serve as reference bases for further analysis and interpretation of the findings. The "Frequencies" subprogram in the *Statistical Package for the Social Sciences* (SPSS)[11] was used to perform this analysis.

Rating of importance of plant location factors

The objective of the analysis in this section is to answer problem one of this study: what is the relative importance of various plant location factors in the eyes of foreign manufacturing investors in the U.S.? The ratings of importance of plant location factors are reported first for all the responding foreign manufacturing investors as a whole and then for each of the major foreign investing countries, SIC codes, employee-size categories, states of plant location, and levels of foreign ownership separately. All together, 39 tables are presented and discussed.[12] The analytical tool used here was also the SPSS "Frequencies" subprogram.[13]

Testing of hypotheses

All the 192 hypotheses were tested using oneway analysis of variance, which was done by use of the "Breakdown" subprogram of SPSS.[14] The null hypothesis to be tested can be stated as: there is no difference among the means of different populations. The alternative hypothesis, which is against the null hypothesis, reads, "At least two population means are different."[15] These hypotheses can be symbolically represented as:

$$H_0 : \mu_1 = \mu_2 = \mu_3 = \ldots \quad (\mu_1, \mu_2, \mu_3 \ldots \text{ are different population means})$$

$$H_1 : \mu_i \neq \mu_j \qquad \text{for at least a pair of i, j}$$
$$\text{(i and j represent different integer values)}$$

Since the magnitude of the difference between population means is expected to be small, a significance level of .10, instead of the more conventional .05, is used. This level is consistent with that advocated by Labovitz, who challenged the use of the .05 level.[16]

Basic dimensions underlying plant location factors

This section of analysis is used to answer the second problem posed in this study: what are the basic "dimensions" or "clusters" underlying this relatively large number of plant location factors? An R-type, varimax-rotated, common factor analysis was performed using the SPSS "Factor" subprogram.[17] Based on the measurement overlaps among the 32 plant location factors, a set of new factors or dimensions are identified. Eigen-values, variations accounted for, and communality values are reported and explained.[18]

Communication sources used by foreign manufacturing investors

A table similar to Table 2-3 is constructed to describe where foreign manufacturing investors got their information in order to decide in which particular community to locate their plant. This part is associated with problem three.

No plant location decision by foreign manufacturers

Based on the data collected from Section I of the questionnaire, some relevant percentage figures are calculated and tables constructed to answer problem four: what percentage and what kinds of foreign manufacturers in the U.S. have not made a plant location decision and why? Here again, the "Frequencies" subprogram was the analytical tool.[19]

CHAPTER IV

FINDINGS

Presented in this chapter are the results of the data analysis. Descriptive statistics and rankings were used to report factual findings. Hypotheses were tested and the underlying dimensions of the 32 plant location factors identified. This information provided a basis from which conclusions and implications of this study were drawn.

GENERAL CHARACTERISTICS OF THE RESPONDING FOREIGN MANUFACTURING INVESTORS

The five descriptive characteristics of the responding firms which returned usable questionnaires and made plant location decisions in the U.S. are: national origin, product category, state of plant location, plant employee size, and degree of foreign ownership.

The nationalities represented by the responding firms are reported in Table 4-1. Over 90 percent of them came from the following eight countries: Germany, United Kingdom, Canada, Japan, France, Switzerland, Sweden, and Netherlands. Nineteen firms were grouped into "other" category, which included such countries as: Austria, Australia, Belgium, Denmark, Finland, Iceland, Italy, and Norway. Comparing Table 4-1 with Table 3-1, which described the distribution of all foreign manufacturing plants in the U.S. over national origin, it appears that this study has a fairly representative group of respondents.

Table 4-2 shows the product category of the plants included in this study. The 224 responding firms were classified into 12 groups by standard industrial classification (SIC) of products produced. The eleven industries which accounted for 81.3 percent of the respondents were: (1) food and kindred products; (2) textile mill products; (3) paper and related products; (4) chemicals and allied products; (5) rubber and plastic products; (6) stone, clay, glass, and concrete products; (7) primary metals; (8) fabricated metal products; (9) industrial machinery; (10) electrical machinery, equipment, and supplies; and (11) measuring, analyzing, and control equipment. Plants in the "other" category were reported to produce such goods as tobacco smoke filters, musical instruments, magnetic tape, cosmetics, and ophthalmic products. The high representativeness of this study's respondents becomes obvious when Table 4-2 is compared with Table 3-2, which presented a distribution of all foreign manufacturing plants in the U.S. over SIC code.

As shown in Table 4-3, seventy percent of the plants included in this study were located in 12 states: Virginia, Georgia, South Carolina, New York,

New Jersey, North Carolina, Pennsylvania, Indiana, Texas, Ohio, Massachusetts, and Illinois. Referring to Table 3-3, foreign manufacturing firms in Virginia, Georgia, and South Carolina were relatively over-represented.

Plants were classified, according to their employee size, into the three categories presented in Table 4-4. The small employee-size plant was originally designed to have 99 or fewer employees. This category accounted for 53 percent of the 215 respondents. Seventy-three plants, representing one third of the respondents, were of medium employee size; this means that the planned number of employees in these plants was between 100 and 499. Twenty-eight firms reported that their plant was built for 500 or more employees.

Based on the degree of non-American ownership in a company, the responding firms were divided into four groups: low, lower-medium, upper-medium, and high. As shown in Table 4-5, over 80 percent of the respondents fell into the high foreign ownership category. The upper-medium foreign ownership category accounted for 12.4 percent of the responding firms. Only 15 firms, or about seven percent of the respondents, reported that they had below-fifty percent foreign ownership in the company.

The respondents were asked, "In what year was the plant location decision made?" As shown in Table 4-6, a little less than 90 percent of them indicated that they made their plant location decision after 1961. Out of a total of 213 plant location decisions, 138, or 65 percent, were actually made after 1971. What this signifies is the high reliability of the survey data, as far as the respondents' memory about their plant location decisions is concerned.

RATINGS OF IMPORTANCE OF PLANT LOCATION FACTORS

The analysis reported in this section is associated with problem one of this study: what is the importance of various plant location factors in the eyes of foreign manufacturing investors in the U.S.? Arithmetic means of respondents' importance ratings were calculated for each of the 32 plant location factors. The mean ratings were then ranked and tabulated from highest to lowest to reveal the relative importance of these factors. The importance ratings of plant location factors are presented in this section in the following order: (1) for all the responding firms as a whole; (2) for each of the eight major foreign investing countries;[1] (3) for each of the 11 major product categories;[2] (4) for each of the 12 major states of plant location;[3] (5) for each of the three employee-size categories;[4] (6) for each of the four foreign-ownership categories.[5] All together, 39 tables are presented and discussed.

Importance of factors for all respondents

Table 4-7 shows the importance ratings of plant location factors for all responding firms. The rank order of mean ratings indicates that the five most influential plant location factors were: (1) availability of transportation services; (2) labor attitudes; (3) ample space for future expansion; (4) nearness to markets within the U.S.; and (5) availability of suitable plant sites. This finding is at odds with Foster's conclusion, which reads:

> . . . the traditional importance the U.S. shipper gives to freight costs, proximity to markets and other practical considerations is not shared by the foreign company. Instead, strategic matters such as long-term availability of raw materials, access to world markets and room for expansion seem to be prime considerations for site location by foreign companies.[6]

The five plant location factors which were rated as least important were: (1) cost of local capital; (2) availability of local capital; (3) nearness to home operation; (4) proximity to export market (outside the U.S.); and (5) nearness to operations in a "third" country.

Importance of factors by major foreign investing countries

For the analysis reported in this section, responses were first classified based on the national origin of the responding firms. Then, mean importance ratings were computed for factors within each of the eight major foreign investing countries.

As shown in Table 4-8, the five most important plant location factors for Canadian manufacturing investors in the U.S. were: (1) availability of transportation services; (2) availability of suitable plant sites; (3) labor attitudes; (4) nearness to markets within the U.S.; and (5) availability of utilities.

Mean importance ratings shown in Table 4-9 indicate that French manufacturing investors regarded the following factors as most influential on locational choices for their plants in the U.S.: (1) nearness to markets within the U.S.; (2) availability of transportation services; (3) ample space for future expansion; (4) labor attitudes; (5) availability of skilled labor; and (6) cost of construction.

As revealed in Table 4-10, German manufacturing investors rated the following five factors highest, on the basis of mean ratings, for the strength of influence exerted on their plant location decisions in the U.S.: (1) labor attitudes; (2) ample space for future expansion; (3) nearness to markets within the U.S.; (4) availability of suitable plant sites; and (5) attitudes of local citizens.

The five plant location factors with highest mean importance ratings for Japanese manufacturers in the U.S., as presented in Table 4-11, were: (1) availability of suitable plant sites; (2) labor attitudes; (3) ample space for future expansion; (4) availability of transportation services; and (5) availability of utilities.

As indicated by the mean ratings in Table 4-12, the five factors rated most important on location decisions for Dutch plants in the U.S. were:

(1) nearness to markets within the U.S.; (2) proximity to raw material sources; (3) availability of transportation services; (4) cost of suitable land; and (5) ample space for future expansion.

The rank order of mean ratings shown in Table 4-13 indicates that Swedish manufacturing investors rated the following factors as most influential on their plant location decisions in the U.S.: (1) availability of transportation services; (2) nearness to markets within the U.S.; (3) labor attitudes; (4) availability of suitable plant sites; (5) cost of transportation services; and (6) cost of suitable land.

As shown in Table 4-14, the following plant location factors were considered most important by Swiss manufacturing investors in the U.S.: (1) availability of transportation services; (2) availability of skilled labor; (3) labor attitudes; (4) cost of suitable land; (5) nearness to markets within the U.S.; and (6) availability of suitable plant sites.

The mean importance ratings shown in Table 4-15 indicate that English manufacturing investors regarded the following five factors as most influential on locational choices for their plants in the U.S.: (1) labor attitudes; (2) availability of transportation services; (3) ample space for future expansion; (4) availability of suitable plant sites; and (5) availability of utilities.

Importance of factors by major product categories

In this section, mean importance ratings for factors were reported in rank order for each of the 11 major product categories.

As revealed in Table 4-16, the following location factors were most important for foreign manufacturing plants producing food and kindred products in the U.S.: (1) availability of suitable plant sites; (2) availability of transportation services; (3) ample space for future expansion; (4) proximity to raw material sources; (5) nearness to markets within the U.S.; (6) proximity to suppliers; (7) labor attitudes; (8) labor laws; (9) cost of transportation services; and (10) cost of construction.

Mean importance ratings by foreign manufacturing investors producing textile mill products were highest, as shown in Table 4-17, for the following plant location factors: (1) nearness to markets within the U.S.; (2) attitudes of local citizens; (3) labor attitudes; (4) labor laws; and (5) availability of transportation services.

As indicated by the mean ratings in Table 4-18, the location factors which were rated most important for plants producing paper and related products were: (1) nearness to markets within the U.S.; (2) availability of suitable plant sites; (3) availability of transportation services; (4) availability of unskilled labor; (5) labor attitudes; and (6) attitudes of local citizens.

The five plant location factors with highest mean ratings for foreign manufacturing plants producing chemicals and allied products, as presented in Table 4-19, were: (1) availability of suitable plant sites; (2) ample space for future expansion; (3) availability of transportation services; (4) availability of utilities; and (5) labor attitudes.

As reported in Table 4-20, the following location factors were most important for foreign manufacturing plants producing rubber and plastic products in the U.S.: (1) availability of transportation services; (2) labor attitudes; (3) labor laws; (4) nearness to markets within the U.S.; (5) availability of utilities; (6) cost of utilities; (7) cost of transportation services; and (8) availability of suitable plant sites.

Mean importance ratings by foreign manufacturing investors producing stone, clay, glass, and concrete products were highest, as shown in Table 4-21, for the following plant location factors: (1) availability of transportation services; (2) ample space for future expansion; (3) availability of utilities; (4) cost of suitable land; and (5) attitudes of government officials.

As indicated by the mean ratings in Table 4-22, the location factors which were rated most important for foreign manufacturing plants producing primary metals were: (1) availability of transportation services; (2) availability of utilities; (3) availability of skilled labor; (4) labor attitudes; (5) cost of utilities; (6) cost of transportation services; and (7) availability of suitable plant sites.

The five location factors with highest mean ratings for foreign manufacturing plants producing fabricated metal products, as presented in Table 4-23, were: (1) labor attitudes; (2) ample space for future expansion; (3) nearness to markets within the U.S.; (4) availability of suitable plant sites; and (5) availability of skilled labor.

As revealed in Table 4-24, the following location factors were most important for foreign manufacturing plants producing industrial machinery in the U.S.: (1) nearness to the markets within the U.S.; (2) availability of transportation services; (3) ample space for future expansion; (4) cost of suitable land; and (5) availability of suitable plant sites.

Mean importance ratings by foreign manufacturing investors producing electrical machinery, equipment, and supplies were highest, as shown in Table 4-25, for the following plant location factors: (1) nearness to markets within the U.S.; (2) labor attitudes; (3) ample space for future expansion; (4) availability of transportation services; (5) availability of managerial and technical personnel; (6) cost of utilities; (7) state tax rates; and (8) attitudes of local citizens.

As indicated by the mean ratings in Table 4-26, the location factors which were rated most important for foreign manufacturing plants producing measuring, analyzing, and control equipment were: (1) labor attitudes; (2) facilities for importing and exporting; (3) availability of transportation services;

(4) availability of managerial and technical personnel; (5) availability of skilled labor; (6) cost of construction; (7) ample space for future expansion; (8) state tax rates; and (9) education facilities.

Importance of factors by major states

For the analysis reported in this section, responses were first classified based on the state of plant locations. Then, mean importance ratings were computed for factors within each of the 12 major states.

The five factors with highest mean ratings for foreign manufacturing plants located in Georgia, as presented in Table 4-27, were: (1) nearness to markets within the U.S.; (2) labor attitudes; (3) availability of suitable plant sites; (4) availability of transportation services; and (5) labor laws.

As shown in Table 4-28, the five most important factors for foreign manufacturing investors in Illinois were: (1) nearness to markets within the U.S.; (2) proximity to suppliers; (3) availability of managerial and technical personnel; (4) availability of skilled labor; and (5) labor attitudes.

The mean importance ratings shown in Table 4-29 indicates that foreign manufacturing investors in Indiana regarded the following factors as most influential on their plant location decisions: (1) nearness to markets within the U.S.; (2) labor attitudes; (3) salary and wage rates; (4) availability of transportation services; (5) ample space for future expansion; and (6) availability of local capital.

As revealed in Table 4-30, foreign manufacturing investors in Massachusetts rated the following factors highest, on the basis of mean ratings, for the strength of influence on their plant location decisions: (1) facilities for importing and exporting; (2) nearness to markets within the U.S.; (3) availability of managerial and technical personnel; (4) labor laws; and (5) ample space for future expansion.

The rank order of mean ratings shown in Table 4-31 indicates that foreign manufacturing investors in New Jersey rated the following factors as most influential on their plant location decisions: (1) availability of transportation services; (2) ample space for future expansion; (3) availability of managerial and technical personnel; (4) availability of skilled labor; (5) nearness to markets within the U.S.; and (6) availability of suitable plant sites.

As shown in Table 4-32, the five most important factors for foreign manufacturing investors in New York were: (1) availability of suitable plant sites; (2) availability of transportation services; (3) ample space for future expansion; (4) labor attitudes; and (5) nearness to markets within the U.S.

The mean importance ratings shown in Table 4-33 indicates that foreign manufacturing investors in North Carolina regarded the following factors as most influential on their plant location decisions: (1) labor attitudes; (2) ample space for future expansion; (3) labor laws; (4) cost of suitable land; (5) availability of suitable plant sites; (6) cost of construction; and (7) attitudes of local citizens.

As revealed in Table 4-34, foreign manufacturing investors in Ohio rated the following factors highest, on the basis of mean ratings, for the strength of influence on their plant location decisions; (1) availability of transportation services; (2) availability of skilled labor; (3) nearness to markets within the U.S.; (4) ample space for future expansion; (5) proximity to suppliers; and (6) availability of utilities.

The rank order of mean ratings shown in Table 4-35 indicates that foreign manufacturing investors in Pennsylvania rated the following factors as most influential on their plant location decisions: (1) nearness to markets within the U.S.; (2) availability of transportation services; (3) availability of suitable plant sites; (4) ample space for future expansion; (5) salary and wage rates; (6) labor attitudes; (7) availability of utilities; (8) cost of transportation services; and (9) cost of suitable land.

As shown in Table 4-36, the six most important plant location factors for foreign manufacturing investors in South Carolina were: (1) nearness to markets within the U.S.; (2) labor attitudes; (3) cost of construction; (4) attitudes of local citizens; (5) labor laws; and (6) ample space for future expansion.

The mean importance ratings shown in Table 4-37 indicates that foreign manufacturing investors in Texas regarded the following factors as most influential on their plant location decisions: (1) availability of transportation services; (2) availability of suitable plant sites; (3) ample space for future expansion; (4) labor attitudes; (5) cost of utilities; and (6) cost of suitable land.

As presented in Table 4-38, foreign manufacturing investors in Virginia rated the following five factors highest, on the basis of mean ratings, for the strength of influence on their plant location decisions: (1) labor attitudes; (2) availability of transportation services; (3) availability of suitable plant sites; (4) ample space for future expansion; and (5) availability of utilities.

Importance of factors by three employee-size categories

In this section, mean importance ratings for factors were reported in rank order for each of the three employee-size groups.

The rank order of mean ratings shown in Table 4-39 indicates that the five location factors which were rated as most influential for small employee-size foreign manufacturing plants in the U.S. were: (1) nearness to markets within the U.S.; (2) availability of transportation services; (3) ample space for future expansion; (4) availability of suitable plant sites; and (5) labor attitudes.

As shown in Table 4-40, the five most important location factors for medium employee size foreign manufacturing plants in the U.S. were: (1) labor attitudes; (2) ample space for future expansion; (3) availability of transportation services; (4) availability of suitable plant sites; and (5) availability of utilities.

The five factors with highest mean importance ratings for large employee size foreign manufacturing plants, as presented in Table 4-41, were: (1) labor attitudes; (2) availability of skilled labor; (3) availability of suitable plant sites; (4) attitudes of local citizens; and (5) availability of transportation services.

Importance of factors by four foreign-ownership categories

For the analysis reported in this section, responses were first classified based on the degree of foreign ownership in the responding firm. Then, mean importance ratings were computed for factors within each of the four foreign-ownership categories.

As presented in Table 4-42, foreign manufacturing investors with a low degree of ownership in a company rated the following five factors highest, on the basis of mean ratings, for the strength of influence on their plant location decisions: (1) labor attitudes; (2) cost of utilities; (3) labor laws; (4) availability of utilities; and (5) availability of transportation services.

The rank order of mean ratings shown in Table 4-43 indicates that the factors which were rated as most influential by foreign manufacturing investors with lower-medium degree of ownership in a company were: (1) labor attitudes; (2) ample space for future expansion; (3) proximity to suppliers; (4) salary and wage rates; (5) availability of transportation services; and (6) availability of suitable plant sites.

As shown in Table 4-44, the most important plant location factors for foreign manufacturing investors with upper-medium degree of ownership in a company were: (1) availability of utilities; (2) nearness to markets within the U.S.; (3) availability of transportation services; (4) availability of suitable plant sites; (5) ample space for future expansion; and (6) attitudes of local citizens.

The five plant location factors with highest mean importance ratings for foreign manufacturing investors with high degree of ownership in a company, as presented in Table 4-45, were: (1) nearness to markets within the U.S.; (2) availability of transportation services; (3) ample space for future expansion; (4) labor attitudes; and (5) availability of suitable plant sites.

Besides the 32 plant location factors listed in the questionnaire, respondents mentioned several other factors which they thought were important. Following is the list of such factors:

1. Size of community
2. Stable and good local economy
3. Labor turnover rate
4. Labor productivity

5. No labor union
6. Nearness to the company's previously established plants
7. Convenience to established sales office
8. Suitability of the area to executives and their families
9. Facilities for children of transferees
10. Social environment for transferees' wives
11. Proximity to hotel accommodations
12. Proximity to restaurants and entertainment
13. Crime levels
14. Good seaport
15. Availability of sewage treatment
16. Availability of good-quality water
17. Along unfrozen sea (in Alaska)

TESTING OF HYPOTHESES

This section presents the test results of the five hypothesis sets, which include 192 hypotheses, described in Chapter I. The one-factor analysis of variance (ANOVA) was used because each hypothesis incorporates three or more population means. The purpose of these tests was to determine if there were significant variations among population means. All hypotheses were tested at the .10 level of significance.

Hypothesis set 1 states that the importance of a plant location factor varies by category of products produced by foreign manufacturers in the U.S. As shown in Table 4-46, significant results were found for the following three factors: (1) proximity to raw material sources; (2) proximity to suppliers; and (3) availability of skilled labor. The mean importance ratings of these three factors, classified by product category, are reported in Table 4-47.

Hypothesis set 2 states that the importance of a plant location factor varies by employee size of foreign manufacturing plants in the U.S. As indicated in Table 4-48, eleven factors showed significant results. They are: (1) facilities for importing and exporting; (2) availability of managerial and technical personnel; (3) availability of skilled labor; (4) availability of unskilled labor; (5) labor attitudes; (6) availability of utilities; (7) cost of utilities; (8) ample space for future expansion; (9) attitudes of government officials; (10) attitudes of local citizens; and (11) housing facilities. The relevant factor mean ratings are shown in Table 4-49.

Hypothesis set 3 states that the importance of a plant location factor varies by location within the U.S. of the foreign manufacturing plants. This hypothesis set was tested at both the state and the regional level. At the state level, significant results were found, as presented in Table 4-50, for the following 15 factors: (1) nearness to markets within the U.S.; (2) nearness to home operation; (3) facilities for importing and exporting; (4) proximity to raw material sources; (5) proximity to suppliers; (6) availability of skilled labor; (7) salary and wage rates; (8) availability of utilities; (9) availability of transportation services; (10) cost of transportation services; (11) availability of suitable plant sites; (12) cost of suitable land; (13) government incentives; (14) attitudes of government officials; and (15) attitudes of local citizens. The mean importance ratings of these 15 factors, classified by state of plant location, are reported in Table 4-51. As revealed in Table 4-52, eleven factors showed significant results at the regional level. They are: (1) proximity to export markets (outside the U.S.); (2) nearness to home operation; (3) proximity to raw material sources; (4) salary and wage rates; (5) labor attitudes; (6) labor laws; (7) availability of utilities; (8) cost of utilities; (9) availability of transportation services; (10) cost of transportation services; and (11) climate. The relevant factor mean ratings are shown in Table 4-53.

Hypothesis set 4 states that the importance of a plant location factor varies by degree of foreign ownership in manufacturing firms in the U.S. As indicated in Table 4-54, significant results were found for the following seven factors: (1) facilities for importing and exporting; (2) proximity to suppliers; (3) salary and wage rates; (4) labor attitudes; (5) cost of utilities; (6) cost of local capital; and (7) government incentives. The mean importance ratings of these seven factors, classified by degree of foreign ownership, are reported in Table 4-55.

Hypothesis set 5 states that the importance of a plant location factor varies by national origin of foreign manufacturing investors in the U.S. The findings are presented in Table 4-56. The six factors which showed significant results are: (1) nearness to home operation; (2) nearness to operations in a "third country"; (3) proximity to raw material sources; (4) salary and wage rates; (5) police and fire protection; and (6) climate. The relevant factor mean ratings are shown in Table 4-57.

BASIC DIMENSIONS UNDERLYING PLANT LOCATION FACTORS

The analysis reported in this section is to answer problem two of this study: what are the basic "dimensions" or "groupings" underlying this relatively large number of plant location factors? Factor analysis is the statistical technique used here.

The results of the factor analysis are summarized in Tables 4-58 and 4-59. Eight dimensions were extracted and were labeled as follows: (1) attitudes of people, labor conditions, and utilities; (2) local capital; (3) suitable land and transportation services; (4) community environment; (5) nearness to supply sources and markets; (6) availability of managerial personnel, and skilled labor; (7) tax rates; and (8) import-export considerations. The eigenvalue of dimension one is much greater than that of any of the other seven dimensions. This is an indication that the first dimension is much more important than the other dimensions.

Three different types of information are provided in Table 4-58: (1) factor loading, which is a measure of correlation between a factor and a dimension;[7] (2) communality, which shows "the degree to which the dimensions account for each of the factors";[8] and (3) eigenvalue, which is the sum of squares of a dimension's factor loadings and is usually used to calculate the fraction of total variance in the factors explained by the dimension.[9] All together, these eight dimensions explain 56 percent of the variation in the 32 plant location factors.[10]

COMMUNICATION SOURCES USED BY FOREIGN MANUFACTURING INVESTORS

Problem three of this study asks: from what sources do foreign manufacturing investors in the U.S. get information in order to decide in which community to locate their plant? As shown in Table 4-60, 18 different information sources were mentioned. Percentagewise, the six most important information sources were: (1) state agencies; (2) local agencies; (3) other firms; (4) outside consultant; (5) U.S. Department of Commerce; and (6) investment missions.

NO PLANT LOCATION DECISION BY FOREIGN MANUFACTURERS

Some foreign manufacturers have never made a plant location decision in the U.S., but they do have a plant here. The analysis presented in this section gives information about how prevalent this situation is, what characteristics this special group of foreign manufacturers possesses, and why this kind of thing could happen. In short, reported in this section are findings associated with problem four posed in this study.

Thirty out of 254, or 11.8 percent of, responding firms which returned usable questionnaires indicated that they had a U.S. plant but had never made a plant location decision. When these 30 firms were asked why they had not made a plant location decision in the U.S., 29 answered they bought an existing firm which owned a plant and one said it leased a U.S. plant. The foreign manufacturing plants in this group typically had a medium or small employee size. No special characteristics were displayed by these 30 firms in terms of product category, state of plant location, and national origin.

SUMMARY

Data collected from the foreign manufacturers surveyed were analyzed. The results of the data analysis were presented in this chapter. First of all, five descriptive characteristics of the responding firms, including national origin, product category, state of plant location, plant employee size, and degree of foreign ownership, were discussed. This information provides a basis for further analysis of the findings.

Next, mean importance ratings of plant location factors and their rank order were reported. Thirty-nine tables were constructed, discussed, and presented in the following order: (1) for all the responding firms as a whole; (2) for each of the eight major foreign investing countries; (3) for each of the 11 major product categories; (4) for each of the 12 major states of plant location; (5) for each of the three employee-size categories; and (6) for each of the four degree-of-foreign-ownership categories. Factors not included in the original 32 plant-location-factor list but which some respondents considered important were reported.

Third, five hypothesis sets, including 192 hypotheses, were tested using the statistical technique of one-factor analysis of variance. Fifty-three hypotheses showed significant results at the .10 significance level. Fourth, an R-type, varimax-rotated, common factor analysis was performed. The eight identified dimensions underlying the 32 plant location factors are: (1) attitudes of people, labor conditions, and utilities; (2) local capital; (3) suitable land and transportation services; (4) community environment; (5) nearness to supply sources and markets; (6) availability of managerial personnel and skilled labor; (7) tax rates; and (8) import-export considerations. Factor loadings, communality values, eigenvalues, and variations accounted for were presented and explained.

The last two sections reported in this chapter are associated with problems 3 and 4 posed in this study. Eighteen different sources from which foreign manufacturing investors got their information to make their plant location decisions in the U.S. were listed. The importance of these information sources was indexed by percentage figures. About 12 percent of the responding firms indicated that they had never made a plant location decision in the U.S., but did have a plant. Two reasons which were given by the respondents to explain this kind of situation were: (1) the company bought an existing firm which owned a plant; and (2) the company leased a U.S. plant. The foreign manufacturing plants in this group typically had a medium or small employee size.

TABLE 4-1
NATIONAL ORIGIN OF THE RESPONDING FIRMS

Country	Number	Percent
Canada	30	13.4
France	21	9.4
Germany	53	23.7
Japan	28	12.5
Netherlands	5	2.2
Sweden	10	4.5
Switzerland	17	7.6
United Kingdom	41	18.3
Other	19	8.4
Total	224	100.0

TABLE 4-2
PRODUCT CATEGORY OF RESPONDENTS' PLANTS

SIC Code	Industry	Number	Percent
20	Food and kindred products	13	5.8
22	Textile mill products	14	6.3
26	Paper and related products	10	4.5
28	Chemicals and allied products	32	14.3
30	Rubber and plastics products	11	4.9
32	Stone, clay, glass, and concrete products	7	3.1
33	Primary metals	6	2.7
34	Fabricated metal products	36	16.1
35	Industrial machinery	30	13.4
36	Electrical machinery, equipment, and supplies	18	8.0
38	Measuring, analyzing, and control equipment	5	2.2
Other		42	18.7
Total		224	100.0

TABLE 4-3
LOCATION OF RESPONDENTS' PLANTS

State	Number	Percent
Georgia	24	10.7
Illinois	5	2.2
Indiana	7	3.1
Massachusetts	5	2.2
New Jersey	15	6.7
New York	18	8.0
North Carolina	15	6.7
Ohio	6	2.7
Pennsylvania	12	5.4
South Carolina	20	8.9
Texas	7	3.1
Virginia	25	11.2
Other	65	29.1
Total	224	100.0

TABLE 4-4
EMPLOYEE-SIZE CATEGORY OF RESPONDENTS' PLANTS

Employee-size Category	Number of Employees	Number of Plants	Percent
Small	99 or less	114	53.0
Medium	100 - 499	73	34.0
Large	500 or more	28	13.0
Total		215	100.0

TABLE 4-5
FOREIGN-OWNERSHIP OF THE RESPONDING FIRMS

Foreign-ownership Category	Percent of Foreign Ownership in the Company	Number of Firms	Percent
Low	10 - 24	7	3.2
Lower-medium	25 - 49	8	3.7
Upper-medium	50 - 74	27	12.4
High	75 - 100	176	80.7
Total		218	100.0

TABLE 4-6
YEAR PLANT LOCATION DECISIONS WERE MADE BY THE RESPONDING FIRMS

Year	Number of Firms	Percent
1901-1950	8	3.8
1951-1960	17	8.0
1961-1970	50	23.5
1971-1977	138	64.7
Total	213	100.0

TABLE 4-7

IMPORTANCE OF PLANT LOCATION FACTORS FOR ALL RESPONDING FIRMS, BY RANK ORDER OF MEAN RATINGS [a]

Factor	Mean Rating	Rank
Availability of transportation services	3.701	1
Labor attitudes	3.665	2
Ample space for future expansion	3.652	3
Nearness to markets within the U.S.	3.647	4
Availability of suitable plant sites	3.594	5
Availability of utilities	3.375	6
Cost of suitable land	3.330	7
Attitudes of local citizens	3.290	8
Cost of construction	3.277	9
Labor laws	3.232	10
Availability of skilled labor	3.192	11
Cost of utilities	3.125	12
Salary and wage rates	3.120	13
Cost of transportation services	3.103	14
State tax rates	3.036	15
Local tax rates	2.982	16
Education facilities	2.938	17
Attitudes of government officials	2.924	18
Availability of managerial and technical personnel	2.911	19
Police and fire protection	2.880	20
Availability of unskilled labor	2.781	21
Housing facilities	2.750	22
Proximity to suppliers	2.741	23
Facilities for importing and exporting	2.656	24
Proximity to raw material sources	2.531	25
Climate	2.375	26
Government incentives	2.321	27
Cost of local capital	2.281	28
Availability of local capital	2.228	29
Nearness to home operation	1.795	30
Proximity to export markets (outside the U.S.)	1.755	31
Nearness to operations in a "third country"	1.219	32

[a] n = 224.

TABLE 4-8

IMPORTANCE OF PLANT LOCATION FACTORS FOR CANADIAN MANUFACTURING INVESTORS, BY RANK ORDER OF MEAN RATING [a]

Factor	Mean Rating	Rank
Availability of transportation services	3.800	1
Availability of suitable plant sites	3.733	2
Labor attitudes	3.667	3
Nearness to markets within the U.S.	3.600	4
Availability of utilities	3.500	5
Ample space for future expansion	3.433	6
Cost of suitable land	3.333	7
Local tax rates	3.300	8
Cost of transportation services	3.300	8
Cost of construction	3.267	10
State tax rates	3.200	11
Labor laws	3.167	12
Attitudes of local citizens	3.133	13
Cost of utilities	3.033	14
Salary and wage rates	3.000	15
Availability of skilled labor	2.967	16
Proximity to raw material sources	2.933	17
Police and fire protection	2.900	18
Attitudes of government officials	2.833	19
Nearness to home operation	2.800	20
Proximity to suppliers	2.800	20
Availability of unskilled labor	2.767	22
Education facilities	2.733	23
Housing facilities	2.633	24
Cost of local capital	2.633	24
Government incentives	2.500	26
Availability of managerial and technical personnel	2.433	27
Facilities for importing and exporting	2.400	28
Availability of local capital	2.367	29
Climate	1.967	30
Proximity to export markets (outside the U.S.)	1.700	31
Nearness to operations in a "third country"	1.200	32

[a] $n = 30$.

TABLE 4-9

IMPORTANCE OF PLANT LOCATION FACTORS FOR FRENCH MANU-
FACTURING INVESTORS, BY RANK ORDER OF MEAN RATINGS [a]

Factor	Mean Rating	Rank
Nearness to markets within the U.S.	3.714	1
Availability of transportation services	3.429	2
Ample space for future expansion	3.429	3
Labor attitudes	3.191	4
Availability of skilled labor	3.095	5
Cost of construction	3.095	5
Cost of utilities	3.000	7
Availability of suitable plant sites	2.952	8
Availability of utilities	2.952	8
State tax rates	2.952	8
Cost of transportation services	2.905	11
Cost of suitable land	2.905	11
Attitudes of local citizens	2.810	13
Salary and wage rates	2.810	13
Labor laws	2.762	15
Local tax rates	2.667	16
Availability of managerial and technical personnel	2.667	16
Proximity to suppliers	2.667	16
Facilities for importing and exporting	2.619	19
Attitudes of government officials	2.524	20
Proximity to raw material sources	2.476	21
Housing facilities	2.429	22
Government incentives	2.429	22
Education facilities	2.333	24
Cost of local capital	2.238	25
Availability of unskilled labor	2.238	25
Police and fire protection	2.143	27
Availability of local capital	2.143	27
Climate	1.810	29
Nearness to home operation	1.714	30
Proximity to export markets (outside the U.S.)	1.619	31
Nearness to operations in a "third country"	1.095	32

[a] n = 21.

TABLE 4-10

IMPORTANCE OF PLANT LOCATION FACTORS FOR GERMAN MANU-
FACTURING INVESTORS, BY RANK ORDER OF MEAN RATINGS [a]

Factor	Mean Rating	Rank
Labor attitudes	3.943	1
Ample space for future expansion	3.887	2
Nearness to markets within the U.S.	3.736	3
Availability of suitable plant sites	3.622	4
Attitudes of local citizens	3.566	5
Labor laws	3.547	6
Cost of suitable land	3.528	7
Availability of transportation services	3.509	8
Cost of construction	3.453	9
Availability of skilled labor	3.453	9
Salary and wage rates	3.453	9
Availability of utilities	3.302	12
Cost of utilities	3.170	13
Education facilities	3.132	14
State tax rates	3.076	15
Police and fire protection	3.057	16
Attitudes of government officials	3.000	17
Housing facilities	2.981	18
Availability of managerial and technical personnel	2.962	19
Cost of transportation services	2.925	20
Local tax rates	2.906	21
Proximity to suppliers	2.830	22
Facilities for importing and exporting	2.793	23
Availability of unskilled labor	2.755	24
Climate	2.462	25
Proximity to raw material sources	2.340	26
Government incentives	2.340	26
Cost of local capital	2.264	28
Availability of local capital	2.170	29
Proximity to export markets (outside the U.S.)	1.962	30
Nearness to home operation	1.679	31
Nearness to operations in a "third country"	1.302	32

[a] n = 53.

TABLE 4-11

IMPORTANCE OF PLANT LOCATION FACTORS FOR JAPANESE MANU-
FACTURING INVESTORS, BY RANK ORDER OF MEAN RATINGS [a]

Factor	Mean Rating	Rank
Availability of suitable plant sites	3.929	1
Labor attitudes	3.786	2
Ample space for future expansion	3.786	2
Availability of transportation services	3.750	4
Availability of utilities	3.679	5
Attitudes of local citizens	3.643	6
Nearness to markets within the U.S.	3.643	6
Attitudes of government officials	3.571	8
Cost of utilities	3.536	9
Cost of suitable land	3.464	10
Salary and wage rates	3.393	11
Cost of construction	3.393	11
Labor laws	3.357	13
Cost of transportation services	3.214	14
Availability of skilled labor	3.179	15
Availability of unskilled labor	3.143	16
Police and fire protection	3.107	17
Availability of managerial and technical personnel	3.107	17
Education facilities	3.107	17
State tax rates	3.071	20
Proximity to raw material sources	3.071	20
Local tax rates	3.071	20
Proximity to suppliers	3.000	23
Housing facilities	2.964	24
Climate	2.821	25
Facilities for importing and exporting	2.536	26
Government incentives	2.464	27
Proximity to export markets (outside the U.S.)	2.000	28
Availability of local capital	1.964	29
Cost of local capital	1.929	30
Nearness to home operation	1.393	31
Nearness to operations in a "third country"	1.179	32

[a] n = 28.

TABLE 4-12

IMPORTANCE OF PLANT LOCATION FACTORS FOR DUTCH MANUFACTURING INVESTORS, BY RANK ORDER OF MEAN RATINGS [a]

Factor	Mean Rating	Rank
Nearness to markets within the U.S.	3.400	1
Proximity to raw material sources	3.400	1
Availability of transportation services	3.400	1
Cost of suitable land	3.200	4
Ample space for future expansion	3.200	4
Availability of suitable plant sites	3.000	6
Cost of utilities	2.800	7
Availability of unskilled labor	2.800	7
Availability of managerial and technical personnel	2.800	7
Availability of skilled labor	2.800	7
Cost of construction	2.800	7
Facilities for importing and exporting	2.800	7
State tax rates	2.600	13
Availability of utilities	2.600	13
Local tax rates	2.600	13
Proximity to suppliers	2.600	13
Labor attitudes	2.400	17
Salary and wage rates	2.400	17
Police and fire protection	2.400	17
Government incentives	2.400	17
Cost of transportation services	2.200	21
Climate	2.200	21
Housing facilities	2.200	21
Labor laws	2.200	21
Education facilities	2.200	21
Cost of local capital	2.200	21
Attitudes of local citizens	2.200	21
Attitudes of government officials	2.200	21
Availability of local capital	1.600	29
Nearness to home operation	1.200	30
Proximity to export markets (outside the U.S.)	1.200	30
Nearness to operations in a "third country"	1.000	32

[a] n = 5.

TABLE 4-13

IMPORTANCE OF PLANT LOCATION FACTORS FOR SWEDISH MANUFACTURING INVESTORS, BY RANK ORDER OF MEAN RATINGS [a]

Factor	Mean Rating	Rank
Availability of transportation services	4.000	1
Nearness to markets within the U.S.	3.600	2
Labor attitudes	3.600	2
Availability of suitable plant sites	3.600	2
Cost of transportation services	3.500	5
Cost of suitable land	3.500	5
Availability of utilities	3.400	7
Ample space for future expansion	3.400	7
State tax rates	3.300	9
Cost of construction	3.200	10
Local tax rates	3.200	10
Availability of skilled labor	3.200	10
Cost of utilities	3.100	13
Labor laws	3.100	13
Availability of managerial and technical personnel	3.000	15
Attitudes of local citizens	2.900	16
Availability of local capital	2.800	17
Cost of local capital	2.800	17
Facilities for importing and exporting	2.800	17
Education facilities	2.700	20
Availability of unskilled labor	2.700	20
Police and fire protection	2.600	22
Climate	2.500	23
Proximity to suppliers	2.500	23
Salary and wage rates	2.400	25
Attitudes of government officials	2.400	25
Proximity to raw material sources	2.300	27
Government incentives	2.200	28
Nearness to home operation	2.200	28
Housing facilities	2.200	28
Nearness to operations in a "third country"	2.000	31
Proximity to export markets (outside the U.S.)	1.900	32

[a] $n = 10$.

TABLE 4-14

IMPORTANCE OF PLANT LOCATION FACTORS FOR SWISS MANUFACTURING INVESTORS, BY RANK ORDER OF MEAN RATINGS [a]

Factor	Mean Rating	Rank
Availability of transportation services	4.059	1
Availability of skilled labor	3.529	2
Labor attitudes	3.529	2
Cost of suitable land	3.529	2
Nearness to markets within the U.S.	3.471	5
Availability of suitable plant sites	3.471	5
Ample space for future expansion	3.412	7
Cost of construction	3.353	8
Availability of utilities	3.294	9
Education facilities	3.294	9
Cost of transportation services	3.235	11
Attitudes of local citizens	3.235	11
Cost of utilities	3.177	13
Labor laws	3.118	14
Police and fire protection	3.059	15
Attitudes of government officials	2.941	16
Housing facilities	2.882	17
Facilities for importing and exporting	2.882	17
Availability of managerial and technical personnel	2.882	17
Local tax rates	2.882	17
Proximity to raw material sources	2.824	21
Salary and wage rates	2.706	22
State tax rates	2.706	22
Climate	2.647	24
Proximity to suppliers	2.647	24
Availability of unskilled labor	2.353	26
Proximity to export markets (outside the U.S.)	2.118	27
Government incentives	2.118	27
Cost of local capital	2.059	29
Availability of local capital	2.059	29
Nearness to home operation	1.824	31
Nearness to operations in a "third country"	1.059	32

[a] n = 17.

TABLE 4-15

IMPORTANCE OF PLANT LOCATION FACTORS FOR ENGLISH MANUFACTURING INVESTORS, BY RANK ORDER OF MEAN RATINGS [a]

Factor	Mean Rating	Rank
Labor attitudes	3.707	1
Availability of transportation services	3.683	2
Ample space for future expansion	3.634	3
Availability of suitable plant sites	3.610	4
Availability of utilities	3.561	5
Nearness to markets within the U.S.	3.537	6
Attitudes of local citizens	3.463	7
Labor laws	3.268	8
Availability of managerial and technical personnel	3.220	9
Availability of skilled labor	3.171	10
Salary and wage rates	3.171	10
Cost of transportation services	3.098	12
Education facilities	3.073	13
Cost of construction	3.049	14
Cost of suitable land	3.024	15
Availability of unskilled labor	3.024	15
Cost of utilities	3.000	17
State tax rates	2.927	18
Local tax rates	2.902	19
Police and fire protection	2.902	19
Attitudes of government officials	2.854	21
Proximity to suppliers	2.756	22
Housing facilities	2.683	23
Facilities for importing and exporting	2.634	24
Availability of local capital	2.293	25
Climate	2.244	26
Cost of local capital	2.244	26
Proximity to raw material sources	2.122	28
Government incentives	2.073	29
Nearness to home operation	1.732	30
Proximity to export markets (outside the U.S.)	1.415	31
Nearness to operations in a "third country"	1.171	32

[a] $n = 41$.

TABLE 4-16

IMPORTANCE OF PLANT LOCATION FACTORS FOR PLANTS
PRODUCING FOOD AND KINDRED PRODUCTS, SIC 20, BY RANK ORDER
OF MEAN RATINGS [a]

Factor	Mean Rating	Rank
Availability of suitable plant sites	4.154	1
Availability of transportation services	4.000	2
Ample space for future expansion	4.000	2
Proximity to raw material sources	3.770	4
Nearness to markets within the U.S.	3.539	5
Proximity to suppliers	3.539	5
Labor attitudes	3.539	5
Labor laws	3.539	5
Cost of transportation services	3.539	5
Cost of construction	3.539	5
Cost of suitable land	3.462	11
Attitudes of local citizens	3.358	12
Availability of utilities	3.308	13
Cost of utilities	3.154	14
Facilities for importing and exporting	3.154	14
Police and fire protection	3.077	16
State tax rates	3.077	16
Local tax rates	3.077	16
Housing facilities	3.000	19
Education facilities	3.000	19
Attitudes of government officials	2.923	21
Government incentives	2.846	22
Salary and wage rates	2.846	22
Availability of managerial and technical personnel	2.770	24
Availability of unskilled labor	2.615	25
Availability of skilled labor	2.615	25
Climate	2.385	27
Availability of local capital	2.077	28
Cost of local capital	2.000	29
Proximity to export markets (outside the U.S.)	1.539	30
Nearness to operations in a "third country"	1.308	31
Nearness to home operation	1.077	32

[a] n = 13.

TABLE 4-17
IMPORTANCE OF PLANT LOCATION FACTORS FOR PLANTS
PRODUCING TEXTILE MILL PRODUCTS, SIC 22, BY RANK ORDER
OF MEAN RATINGS [a]

Factor	Mean Rating	Rank
Nearness to markets within the U.S.	3.857	1
Attitudes of local citizens	3.714	2
Labor attitudes	3.643	3
Labor laws	3.429	4
Availability of transportation services	3.429	4
Availability of suitable plant sites	3.357	6
Education facilities	3.286	7
Availability of managerial and technical personnel	3.214	8
Availability of utilities	3.214	8
Ample space for future expansion	3.214	8
Attitudes of government officials	3.143	11
Local tax rates	3.143	11
State tax rates	3.071	11
Availability of skilled labor	3.071	14
Availability of unskilled labor	3.000	14
Salary and wage rates	3.000	16
Cost of utilities	3.000	16
Climate	3.000	16
Cost of construction	2.929	19
Housing facilities	2.857	20
Cost of suitable land	2.857	20
Police and fire protection	2.857	20
Cost of transportation services	2.714	23
Proximity to suppliers	2.714	23
Proximity to raw material sources	2.643	25
Facilities for importing and exporting	2.500	26
Government incentives	2.429	27
Availability of local capital	2.357	28
Cost of local capital	2.286	29
Proximity to export markets (outside the U.S.)	1.571	30
Nearness to home operation	1.500	31
Nearness to operations in a "third country"	1.143	32

[a] n = 14.

TABLE 4-18

IMPORTANCE OF PLANT LOCATION FACTORS FOR PLANTS
PRODUCING PAPER AND RELATED PRODUCTS, SIC 26, BY RANK
ORDER OF MEAN RATINGS [a]

Factor	Mean Rating	Rank
Nearness to markets within the U.S.	4.000	1
Availability of suitable plant sites	3.600	2
Availability of transportation services	3.500	3
Availability of unskilled labor	3.400	4
Labor attitudes	3.400	4
Attitudes of local citizens	3.400	4
Ample space for future expansion	3.300	7
Police and fire protection	3.100	8
Proximity to suppliers	3.100	8
Cost of suitable land	3.000	10
Labor laws	3.000	10
Availability of managerial and technical personnel	2.900	12
Availablity of utilities	2.900	12
Facilities for importing and exporting	2.800	14
Education facilities	2.800	14
Cost of construction	2.800	14
Proximity to raw material sources	2.700	17
Salary and wage rates	2.700	17
Cost of utilities	2.700	17
Availability of skilled labor	2.700	17
Housing facilities	2.700	17
Cost of transportation services	2.700	17
Attitudes of government officials	2.600	23
State tax rates	2.500	24
Local tax rates	2.400	25
Cost of local capital	2.000	26
Availability of local capital	1.900	27
Government incentives	1.800	28
Proximity to export markets (outside the U.S.)	1.800	28
Nearness to home operation	1.700	30
Climate	1.600	31
Nearness to operations in a "third country"	1.100	32

[a] n = 10.

TABLE 4-19

IMPORTANCE OF PLANT LOCATION FACTORS FOR PLANTS PRODUCING CHEMICALS AND ALLIED PRODUCTS, SIC 28, BY RANK ORDER OF MEAN RATINGS [a]

Factor	Mean Rating	Rank
Availability of suitable plant sites	4.000	1
Ample space for future expansion	4.000	1
Availability of transportation services	3.875	3
Availability of utilities	3.844	4
Labor attitudes	3.656	5
Cost of suitable land	3.625	6
Cost of construction	3.625	6
Nearness to markets within the U.S.	3.500	8
Attitudes of local citizens	3.406	9
Cost of utilities	3.344	10
Education facilities	3.188	11
Proximity to raw material sources	3.188	11
Labor laws	3.156	13
Cost of transportation services	3.125	14
Availability of skilled labor	3.094	15
Attitudes of government officials	3.031	16
Police and fire protection	2.969	17
Availability of managerial and technical personnel	2.969	17
State tax rates	2.938	19
Local tax rates	2.875	20
Salary and wage rates	2.844	21
Housing facilities	2.750	22
Facilities for importing and exporting	2.750	22
Availablity of unskilled labor	2.500	24
Proximity to suppliers	2.438	25
Climate	2.406	26
Nearness to home operation	1.875	27
Proximity to export markets (outside the U.S.)	1.875	27
Government incentives	1.813	29
Cost of local capital	1.750	30
Availability of local capital	1.656	31
Nearness to operations in a "third country"	1.188	32

[a] n = 32.

TABLE 4-20

IMPORTANCE OF PLANT LOCATION FACTORS FOR PLANTS PRODUCING RUBBER AND PLASTIC PRODUCTS, SIC 30, BY RANK ORDER OF MEAN RATINGS [a]

Factor	Mean Rating	Rank
Availability of transportation services	3.818	1
Labor attitudes	3.636	2
Labor laws	3.636	2
Nearness to markets within the U.S.	3.455	4
Availability of utilities	3.364	5
Cost of utilities	3.364	5
Cost of transportation services	3.364	5
Availability of suitable plant sites	3.364	5
Ample space for future expansion	3.182	9
Availability of managerial and technical personnel	3.000	10
Salary and wage rates	3.000	10
Cost of suitable land	3.000	10
Availability of skilled labor	2.909	13
Local tax rates	2.909	13
Cost of construction	2.909	13
State tax rates	2.818	16
Proximity to raw material sources	2.727	17
Attitudes of local citizens	2.727	17
Attitudes of government officials	2.636	19
Police and fire protection	2.546	20
Availability of unskilled labor	2.546	20
Proximity to suppliers	2.546	20
Climate	2.364	23
Education facilities	2.273	24
Housing facilities	2.091	25
Government incentives	2.000	26
Cost of local capital	1.909	27
Availability of local capital	1.818	28
Facilities for importing and exporting	1.727	29
Proximity to export markets (outside the U.S.)	1.636	30
Nearness to home operation	1.455	31
Nearness to operations in a "third country"	1.182	32

[a] $n = 11$.

TABLE 4-21

IMPORTANCE OF PLANT LOCATION FACTORS FOR PLANTS PRODUCING STONE, CLAY, GLASS, AND CONCRETE PRODUCTS, SIC 32, BY RANK ORDER OF MEAN RATINGS [a]

Factor	Mean Rating	Rank
Availability of transportation services	4.143	1
Ample space for future expansion	4.143	1
Availability of utilities	4.000	3
Cost of suitable land	4.000	3
Attitudes of government officials	4.000	3
Attitudes of local citizens	3.857	6
Availability of suitable plant sites	3.857	6
Salary and wage rates	3.857	6
Cost of construction	3.714	9
Cost of utilities	3.714	9
Local tax rates	3.571	11
State tax rates	3.571	11
Labor attitudes	3.571	11
Cost of transportation services	3.429	14
Availability of unskilled labor	3.286	15
Nearness to markets within the U.S.	3.143	16
Cost of local capital	3.143	16
Government incentives	3.143	16
Labor laws	3.143	16
Education facilities	2.857	20
Police and fire protection	2.714	21
Availability of local capital	2.714	21
Proximity to raw material sources	2.714	21
Housing facilities	2.571	24
Facilities for importing and exporting	2.429	25
Climate	2.286	26
Availability of managerial and technical personnel	2.286	26
Availability of skilled labor	2.286	26
Proximity to suppliers	2.000	29
Proximity to export markets (outside the U.S.)	1.857	30
Nearness to home operation	1.857	30
Nearness to operations in a "third country"	1.429	32

[a] n = 7.

TABLE 4-22

IMPORTANCE OF PLANT LOCATION FACTORS FOR PLANTS PRODUCING PRIMARY METALS, SIC 33, BY RANK ORDER OF MEAN RATINGS [a]

Factor	Mean Rating	Rank
Availability of transportation services	4.333	1
Availability of utilities	4.000	2
Availability of skilled labor	3.833	3
Labor attitudes	3.667	4
Cost of utilities	3.667	4
Cost of transportation services	3.667	4
Availability of suitable plant sites	3.667	4
Ample space for future expansion	3.500	8
Cost of suitable land	3.333	9
Nearness to markets within the U.S.	3.167	10
Proximity to suppliers	3.167	10
Salary and wage rates	3.167	10
Labor laws	3.000	13
Government incentives	2.833	14
Attitudes of local citizens	2.833	14
Proximity to raw material sources	2.833	14
Cost of construction	2.667	17
State tax rates	2.667	17
Facilities for importing and exporting	2.500	19
Cost of local capital	2.500	19
Availability of local capital	2.500	19
Local tax rates	2.500	19
Attitudes of government officials	2.500	19
Police and fire protection	2.333	24
Availability of mangerial and technical personnel	2.333	24
Availability of unskilled labor	2.333	24
Nearness to home operation	2.167	27
Housing facilities	2.167	27
Education facilities	2.167	27
Proximity to export markets (outside the U.S.)	2.000	30
Climate	2.000	30
Nearness to operations in a "third country"	1.333	32

[a] n = 6.

TABLE 4-23

IMPORTANCE OF PLANT LOCATION FACTORS FOR PLANTS PRODUCING FABRICATED METAL PRODUCTS, SIC 34, BY RANK ORDER OF MEAN RATINGS [a]

Factor	Mean Rating	Rank
Labor attitudes	4.056	1
Ample space for future expansion	3.778	2
Nearness to markets within the U.S.	3.667	3
Availability of suitable plant sites	3.528	4
Availability of skilled labor	3.472	5
Attitudes of local citizens	3.444	6
Availability of transportation services	3.444	7
Cost of suitable land	3.417	8
Availability of utilities	3.361	9
Cost of construction	3.278	10
Labor laws	3.222	11
Salary and wage rates	3.194	12
State tax rates	3.167	13
Availability of unskilled labor	3.111	14
Cost of utilities	3.028	15
Local tax rates	3.000	16
Attitudes of government officials	2.944	17
Cost of transportation services	2.917	18
Education facilities	2.833	19
Housing facilities	2.750	20
Police and fire protection	2.694	21
Availability of local capital	2.639	22
Availability of managerial and technical personnel	2.472	23
Proximity to suppliers	2.444	24
Cost of local capital	2.417	25
Government incentives	2.278	26
Facilities for importing and exporting	2.194	27
Proximity to raw material sources	2.111	28
Climate	2.111	28
Nearness to home operation	2.028	30
Proximity to export markets (outside the U.S.)	1.528	31
Nearness to operations in a "third country"	1.167	32

[a] n = 36.

TABLE 4-24

**IMPORTANCE OF PLANT LOCATION FACTORS FOR PLANTS
PRODUCING INDUSTRIAL MACHINERY, SIC 35, BY RANK ORDER
OF MEAN RATINGS [a]**

Factor	Mean Rating	Rank
Nearness to markets within the U.S.	4.100	1
Availability of transportation services	3.767	2
Ample space for future expansion	3.733	3
Cost of suitable land	3.533	4
Availability of suitable plant sites	3.433	5
Availability of skilled labor	3.400	6
Labor attitudes	3.367	7
Cost of construction	3.367	7
Labor laws	3.233	9
Salary and wage rates	3.167	10
Availability of utilities	3.167	10
Attitudes of local citizens	3.000	12
Education facilities	2.967	13
Cost of utilities	2.967	13
Cost of transportation services	2.967	13
State tax rates	2.967	13
Local tax rates	2.933	17
Proximity to suppliers	2.900	18
Facilities for importing and exporting	2.900	18
Availability of managerial and technical personnel	2.900	18
Police and fire protection	2.900	18
Housing facilities	2.867	22
Attitudes of government officials	2.667	23
Climate	2.467	24
Cost of local capital	2.433	25
Availability of unskilled labor	2.400	26
Government incentives	2.200	27
Proximity to raw material sources	2.167	28
Availability of local capital	2.067	29
Proximity to export markets (outside the U.S.)	1.933	30
Nearness to home operation	1.600	31
Nearness to operations in a "third country"	1.067	32

[a] $n = 30$.

TABLE 4-25

IMPORTANCE OF PLANT LOCATION FACTORS FOR PLANTS PRODUCING ELECTRICAL MACHINERY, EQUIPMENT, AND SUPPLIES, SIC 36, BY RANK ORDER OF MEAN RATINGS [a]

Factor	Mean Rating	Rank
Nearness to markets within the U.S.	3.611	1
Labor attitudes	3.556	2
Ample space for future expansion	3.444	3
Availability of transportation services	3.389	4
Availability of managerial and technical personnel	3.278	5
Cost of utilities	3.278	5
State tax rates	3.278	5
Attitudes of local citizens	3.278	5
Availability of skilled labor	3.222	9
Salary and wage rates	3.222	9
Cost of transportation services	3.222	9
Local tax rates	3.222	9
Labor laws	3.111	13
Availability of utilities	3.111	13
Police and fire protection	3.056	15
Cost of construction	3.056	15
Availability of suitable plant sites	3.000	17
Cost of suitable land	3.000	17
Education facilities	3.000	17
Proximity to suppliers	2.944	20
Housing facilities	2.944	20
Attitudes of government officials	2.889	22
Availability of unskilled labor	2.722	23
Facilities for importing and exporting	2.556	24
Government incentives	2.556	24
Cost of local capital	2.500	26
Availability of local capital	2.444	27
Climate	2.333	28
Proximity to raw material sources	2.167	29
Nearness to home operation	2.000	30
Proximity to export markets (outside the U.S.)	1.556	31
Nearness to operations in a "third country"	1.389	32

[a] n = 18.

TABLE 4-26

IMPORTANCE OF PLANT LOCATION FACTORS FOR PLANTS
PRODUCING MEASURING, ANALYZING, AND CONTROL EQUIPMENT,
SIC 38, BY RANK ORDER OF MEAN RATINGS [a]

Factor	Mean Rating	Rank
Labor attitudes	3.800	1
Facilities for importing and exporting	3.600	2
Availability of transportation services	3.600	2
Availability of managerial and technical personnel	3.400	4
Availability of skilled labor	3.400	4
Cost of construction	3.400	4
Ample space for future expansion	3.400	4
State tax rates	3.400	4
Education facilities	3.400	4
Availability of unskilled labor	3.200	10
Nearness to markets within the U.S.	3.200	10
Salary and wage rates	3.200	10
Availability of utilities	3.200	10
Cost of local capital	3.200	10
Availability of suitable plant sites	3.200	10
Local tax rates	3.200	10
Attitudes of local citizens	3.200	10
Housing facilities	3.200	10
Proximity to suppliers	3.000	19
Cost of utilities	3.000	19
Police and fire protection	3.000	19
Availability of local capital	3.000	19
Cost of suitable land	2.800	23
Climate	2.800	23
Government incentives	2.600	25
Labor laws	2.600	25
Nearness to home operation	2.600	25
Cost of transportation services	2.400	28
Attitudes of government officials	2.400	28
Proximity to raw material sources	2.200	30
Proximity to export markets (outside the U.S.)	2.000	31
Nearness to operations in a "third country"	1.800	32

[a] n = 5.

TABLE 4-27

IMPORTANCE OF PLANT LOCATION FACTORS FOR FOREIGN MANUFACTURING INVESTORS IN GEORGIA, BY RANK ORDER OF MEAN RATINGS [a]

Factor	Mean Rating	Rank
Nearness to markets within the U.S.	4.000	1
Labor attitudes	3.958	2
Availability of suitable plant sites	3.917	3
Availability of transportation services	3.875	4
Labor laws	3.583	5
Ample space for future expansion	3.542	6
Salary and wage rates	3.500	7
Cost of suitable land	3.458	8
Availability of utilities	3.333	9
Cost of transportation services	3.208	10
Cost of utilities	3.125	11
Attitudes of local citizens	3.125	11
State tax rates	3.125	11
Cost of construction	3.125	11
Availability of skilled labor	3.083	15
Availability of unskilled labor	3.042	16
Local tax rates	3.000	17
Attitudes of government officials	2.917	18
Availability of managerial and technical personnel	2.917	18
Police and fire protection	2.792	20
Education facilities	2.750	21
Proximity to suppliers	2.750	21
Proximity to raw material sources	2.708	23
Climate	2.583	24
Housing facilities	2.542	25
Availability of local capital	2.458	26
Cost of local capital	2.375	27
Government incentives	2.292	28
Facilities for importing and exporting	2.208	29
Proximity to export markets (outside the U.S.)	1.500	30
Nearness to operations in a "third country"	1.333	31
Nearness to home operation	1.250	32

[a] $n = 24$.

TABLE 4-28

IMPORTANCE OF PLANT LOCATION FACTORS FOR FOREIGN MANUFACTURING INVESTORS IN ILLINOIS, BY RANK ORDER OF MEAN RATINGS [a]

Factors	Mean Rating	Rank
Nearness to markets within the U.S.	3.200	1
Proximity to suppliers	2.800	2
Availability of managerial and technical personnel	2.800	2
Availability of skilled labor	2.800	2
Labor attitudes	2.800	2
Ample space for future expansion	2.400	6
Labor laws	2.400	6
Cost of construction	2.400	6
State tax rates	2.400	6
Local tax rates	2.200	10
Availability of unskilled labor	2.200	10
Availability of transportation services	2.200	10
Cost of suitable land	2.200	10
Police and fire protection	2.000	14
Cost of utilities	2.000	14
Salary and wage rates	1.800	16
Availability of suitable plant sites	1.800	16
Attitudes of local citizens	1.800	16
Climate	1.600	19
Housing facilities	1.600	19
Cost of transportation services	1.600	19
Education facilities	1.600	19
Proximity to raw material sources	1.600	19
Availability of utilities	1.600	19
Cost of local capital	1.600	19
Facilities for importing and exporting	1.600	19
Nearness to home operation	1.600	19
Availability of local capital	1.400	28
Attitudes of government officials	1.200	29
Proximity to export markets (outside the U.S.)	1.200	29
Government incentives	1.200	29
Nearness to operations in a "third country"	1.000	32

[a] n = 5.

TABLE 4-29

IMPORTANCE OF PLANT LOCATION FACTORS FOR FOREIGN MANUFACTURING INVESTORS IN INDIANA, BY RANK ORDER OF MEAN RATINGS [a]

Factor	Mean Rating	Rank
Nearness to markets within the U.S.	4.143	1
Labor attitudes	3.429	2
Salary and wage rates	3.286	3
Availability of transportation services	3.286	3
Ample space for future expansion	3.286	3
Availability of local capital	3.286	3
Attitudes of local citizens	3.143	7
Attitudes of government officials	3.143	7
Cost of utilities	3.143	7
Availability of utilities	3.000	10
Education facilities	3.000	10
Police and fire protection	3.000	10
Availability of suitable plant sites	3.000	10
Cost of suitable land	3.000	10
Cost of construction	2.857	15
State tax rates	2.857	15
Housing facilities	2.857	15
Cost of transportation services	2.714	18
Availability of unskilled labor	2.714	18
Local tax rates	2.714	18
Availability of managerial and technical personnel	2.571	21
Labor laws	2.571	21
Proximity to suppliers	2.429	23
Availability of skilled labor	2.429	23
Proximity to raw material sources	2.286	25
Cost of local capital	2.143	26
Facilities for importing and exporting	2.000	27
Government incentives	2.000	27
Climate	1.857	29
Proximity to export markets (outside the U.S.)	1.571	30
Nearness to home operation	1.286	31
Nearness to operations in a "third country"	1.000	32

[a] n = 7.

TABLE 4-30

IMPORTANCE OF PLANT LOCATION FACTORS FOR FOREIGN
MANUFACTURING INVESTORS IN MASSACHUSETTS, BY RANK ORDER
OF MEAN RATINGS [a]

Factor	Mean Rating	Rank
Facilities for importing and exporting	3.400	1
Nearness to markets within the U.S.	3.200	2
Availability of managerial and technical personnel	3.000	3
Labor laws	3.000	3
Ample space for future expansion	3.000	3
Availability of transportation services	2.800	6
Cost of utilities	2.800	6
Availability of skilled labor	2.800	6
Availability of suitable plant sites	2.800	6
Labor attitudes	2.800	6
Education facilities	2.400	11
State tax rates	2.400	11
Availability of utilities	2.400	11
Cost of transportation services	2.400	11
Housing facilities	2.400	11
Local tax rates	2.400	11
Cost of construction	2.200	17
Proximity to suppliers	2.000	18
Government incentives	2.000	18
Police and fire protection	2.000	18
Attitudes of local citizens	2.000	18
Salary and wage rates	2.000	18
Attitudes of government officials	2.000	18
Cost of suitable land	1.800	24
Climate	1.600	25
Availability of unskilled labor	1.600	25
Cost of local capital	1.600	25
Nearness to home operation	1.400	28
Availability of local capital	1.400	28
Nearness to operations in a "third country"	1.000	30
Proximity to export markets (outside the U.S.)	1.000	30
Proximity to raw material sources	1.000	30

[a] $n = 5$.

TABLE 4-31

IMPORTANCE OF PLANT LOCATION FACTORS FOR FOREIGN MANUFACTURING INVESTORS IN NEW JERSEY, BY RANK ORDER OF MEAN RATINGS [a]

Factor	Mean Rating	Rank
Availability of transportation services	3.733	1
Ample space for future expansion	3.733	1
Availability of managerial and technical personnel	3.600	3
Availability of skilled labor	3.400	4
Nearness to markets within the U.S.	3.333	5
Availability of suitable plant sites	3.333	5
Cost of construction	3.267	7
Facilities for importing and exporting	3.267	7
Cost of suitable land	3.200	9
Proximity to suppliers	3.133	10
Availability of utilities	3.133	10
Labor attitudes	3.000	12
Attitudes of local citizens	3.000	12
Cost of transportation services	3.000	12
Education facilities	3.000	12
Police and fire protection	3.000	12
Salary and wage rates	2.800	17
Cost of utilities	2.733	18
State tax rates	2.733	18
Availability of unskilled labor	2.667	20
Labor laws	2.667	20
Nearness to home operation	2.600	22
Local tax rates	2.533	23
Housing facilities	2.467	24
Attitudes of government officials	2.400	25
Cost of local capital	2.333	26
Proximity to raw material sources	2.267	27
Availability of local capital	2.200	28
Climate	2.133	29
Government incentives	1.667	30
Proximity to export markets (outside the U.S.)	1.667	30
Nearness to operations in a "third country"	1.133	32

[a] n = 15.

TABLE 4-32

IMPORTANCE OF PLANT LOCATION FACTORS FOR FOREIGN
MANUFACTURING INVESTORS IN NEW YORK, BY RANK ORDER OF
MEAN RATINGS [a]

Factor	Mean Rating	Rank
Availability of suitable plant sites	3.778	1
Availability of transportation services	3.772	2
Ample space for future expansion	3.667	3
Labor attitudes	3.611	4
Nearness to markets within the U.S.	3.500	5
Cost of transportation services	3.389	6
Attitudes of local citizens	3.389	6
Cost of construction	3.389	6
Availability of utilities	3.333	9
Cost of suitable land	3.333	9
Climate	3.278	11
Attitudes of government officials	3.278	11
Cost of utilities	3.222	13
Education facilities	3.222	13
Police and fire protection	3.222	13
Nearness to home operation	3.167	16
Labor laws	3.167	16
Local tax rates	3.111	18
Housing facilities	3.111	18
Facilities for importing and exporting	3.111	18
Government incentives	3.056	21
Salary and wage rates	3.000	22
Availability of skilled labor	2.889	23
Cost of local capital	2.833	24
State tax rates	2.833	24
Availability of local capital	2.722	26
Availability of managerial and technical personnel	2.722	26
Availability of unskilled labor	2.611	28
Proximity to suppliers	2.444	29
Proximity to raw material sources	2.167	30
Proximity to export markets (outside the U.S.)	1.944	31
Nearness to operations in a "third country"	1.500	32

[a] $n = 18$.

TABLE 4-33

IMPORTANCE OF PLANT LOCATION FACTORS FOR FOREIGN
MANUFACTURING INVESTORS IN NORTH CAROLINA, BY RANK
ORDER OF MEAN RATINGS [a]

Factor	Mean Rating	Rank
Labor attitudes	3.867	1
Ample space for future expansion	3.867	1
Labor laws	3.800	3
Cost of suitable land	3.733	4
Availability of suitable plant sites	3.667	5
Cost of construction	3.667	5
Attitudes of local citizens	3.667	5
Availability of transportation services	3.533	8
Salary and wage rates	3.533	8
Availability of utilities	3.467	10
Availability of skilled labor	3.467	10
Availability of unskilled labor	3.467	10
Nearness to markets within the U.S.	3.333	13
Attitudes of government officials	3.333	13
Education facilities	3.200	15
Cost of utilities	3.133	16
Police and fire protection	3.067	17
Local tax rates	3.067	17
Cost of transportation services	3.000	19
State tax rates	3.000	19
Climate	2.800	21
Housing facilities	2.800	21
Availability of managerial and technical personnel	2.467	23
Availability of local capital	2.267	24
Cost of local capital	2.267	24
Proximity to suppliers	2.267	26
Government incentives	2.133	27
Facilities for importing and exporting	2.133	27
Proximity to raw material sources	1.867	29
Nearness to home operation	1.667	30
Proximity to export markets (outside the U.S.)	1.467	31
Nearness to operations in a "third country"	1.067	32

[a] n = 15.

TABLE 4-34

IMPORTANCE OF PLANT LOCATION FACTORS FOR FOREIGN MANUFACTURING INVESTORS IN OHIO, BY RANK ORDER OF MEAN RATINGS [a]

Factor	Mean Rating	Rank
Availability of transportation services	4.667	1
Availability of skilled labor	4.500	2
Nearness to markets within the U.S.	4.333	3
Ample space for future expansion	4.167	4
Proximity to suppliers	4.000	5
Availability of utilities	4.000	5
Labor attitudes	3.833	7
Availability of suitable plant sites	3.833	7
Cost of suitable land	3.667	9
Cost of transportation services	3.500	10
Labor laws	3.333	11
Cost of utilities	3.167	12
State tax rates	3.167	12
Proximity to raw material sources	3.000	14
Availability of managerial and technical personnel	3.000	14
Cost of construction	3.000	14
Attitudes of local citizens	3.000	14
Salary and wage rates	3.000	14
Education facilities	3.000	14
Police and fire protection	3.000	14
Housing facilities	2.833	21
Local tax rates	2.667	22
Facilities for importing and exporting	2.667	22
Cost of local capital	2.167	24
Availability of unskilled labor	2.000	25
Nearness to home operation	2.000	25
Climate	2.000	25
Attitudes of government officials	2.000	25
Proximity to export markets (outside the U.S.)	1.833	29
Availability of local capital	1.833	29
Government incentives	1.667	31
Nearness to operations in a "third country"	1.500	32

[a] n = 6.

TABLE 4-35

IMPORTANCE OF PLANT LOCATION FACTORS FOR FOREIGN MANUFACTURING INVESTORS IN PENNSYLVANIA, BY RANK ORDER OF MEAN RATINGS [a]

Factor	Mean Rating	Rank
Nearness to markets within the U.S.	3.667	1
Availability of transportation services	3.667	1
Availability of suitable plant sites	3.583	3
Ample space for future expansion	3.583	3
Salary and wage rates	3.500	5
Labor attitudes	3.500	5
Availability of utilities	3.500	5
Cost of transportation services	3.500	5
Cost of suitable land	3.500	5
Availability of skilled labor	3.416	10
Attitudes of local citizens	3.416	10
Cost of construction	3.333	12
Local tax rates	3.333	12
Attitudes of government officials	3.333	12
Cost of utilities	3.167	15
Labor laws	3.083	16
State tax rates	3.083	16
Government incentives	3.000	18
Police and fire protection	2.916	19
Availability of unskilled labor	2.833	20
Availability of managerial and technical personnel	2.833	20
Education facilities	2.750	22
Housing facilities	2.583	23
Proximity to suppliers	2.500	24
Facilities for importing and exporting	2.333	25
Climate	2.250	26
Cost of local capital	2.167	27
Proximity to raw material sources	2.000	28
Availability of local capital	1.917	29
Nearness to home operation	1.583	30
Proximity to export markets (outside the U.S.)	1.417	31
Nearness to operations in a "third country"	1.083	32

[a] $n = 12$.

TABLE 4-36

IMPORTANCE OF PLANT LOCATION FACTORS FOR FOREIGN
MANUFACTURING INVESTORS IN SOUTH CAROLINA, BY RANK ORDER
OF MEAN RATINGS [a]

Factor	Mean Rating	Rank
Nearness to markets within the U.S.	4.300	1
Labor attitudes	3.850	2
Cost of construction	3.800	3
Attitudes of local citizens	3.800	3
Labor laws	3.700	5
Ample space for future expansion	3.700	5
Cost of suitable land	3.600	7
Availability of transportation services	3.600	7
Salary and wage rates	3.550	9
Education facilities	3.550	9
Availability of skilled labor	3.500	11
Availability of suitable plant sites	3.450	12
Housing facilities	3.250	13
State tax rates	3.200	14
Availability of managerial and technical personnel	3.150	15
Facilities for importing and exporting	3.150	15
Availability of utilities	3.100	17
Local tax rates	3.000	18
Attitudes of government officials	3.000	18
Proximity to suppliers	2.900	20
Cost of utilities	2.900	20
Police and fire protection	2.800	22
Climate	2.700	23
Cost of transportation services	2.700	23
Availability of unskilled labor	2.650	25
Proximity to raw material sources	2.500	26
Government incentives	2.300	27
Proximity to export markets (outside the U.S.)	2.150	28
Availability of local capital	2.000	29
Cost of local capital	2.000	29
Nearness to home operation	1.200	31
Nearness to operations in a "third country"	1.000	32

[a] n = 20.

TABLE 4-37

IMPORTANCE OF PLANT LOCATION FACTORS FOR FOREIGN MANUFACTURING INVESTORS IN TEXAS, BY RANK ORDER OF MEAN RATINGS [a]

Factor	Mean Rating	Rank
Availability of transportation services	4.286	1
Availability of suitable plant sites	4.143	2
Ample space for future expansion	4.143	2
Labor attitudes	4.000	4
Cost of utilities	4.000	4
Cost of suitable land	4.000	4
Availability of utilities	3.857	7
Availability of skilled labor	3.714	8
Local tax rates	3.714	8
Cost of construction	3.714	8
Cost of transportation services	3.429	11
Attitudes of local citizens	3.429	11
Proximity to raw material sources	3.429	11
Nearness to markets within the U.S.	3.286	14
Availability of managerial and technical personnel	3.286	14
Labor laws	3.286	14
Salary and wage rates	3.286	14
Housing facilities	3.143	18
Education facilities	3.143	18
Attitudes of government officials	3.143	18
Police and fire protection	3.000	21
Proximity to suppliers	2.857	22
Availability of unskilled labor	2.714	23
State tax rates	2.571	24
Climate	2.286	25
Facilities for importing and exporting	2.143	26
Availability of local capital	2.143	26
Cost of local capital	2.143	26
Nearness to home operation	1.857	29
Government incentives	1.714	30
Proximity to export markets (outside the U.S.)	1.286	31
Nearness to operations in a "third country"	1.000	32

[a] $n = 7$.

TABLE 4-38

IMPORTANCE OF PLANT LOCATION FACTORS FOR FOREIGN
MANUFACTURING INVESTORS IN VIRGINIA, BY RANK ORDER
OF MEAN RATINGS [a]

Factor	Mean Rating	Rank
Labor attitudes	4.080	1
Availability of transportation services	3.840	2
Availability of suitable plant sites	3.800	3
Ample space for future expansion	3.680	4
Availability of utilities	3.520	5
Labor laws	3.480	6
Cost of suitable land	3.480	6
Nearness to markets within the U.S.	3.400	8
Attitudes of local citizens	3.360	9
Proximity to suppliers	3.320	10
Police and fire protection	3.320	10
Cost of transportation services	3.200	12
Cost of construction	3.160	13
Facilities for importing and exporting	3.120	14
Education facilities	3.120	14
State tax rates	3.120	14
Salary and wage rates	3.080	17
Housing facilities	3.040	18
Cost of utilities	3.040	18
Local tax rates	3.040	18
Availability of skilled labor	3.000	21
Availability of unskilled labor	2.920	22
Attitudes of government officials	2.920	22
Climate	2.760	24
Availability of managerial and technical personnel	2.680	25
Government incentives	2.360	26
Availability of local capital	2.200	27
Cost of local capital	2.200	27
Proximity to raw material sources	1.920	29
Proximity to export markets (outside the U.S.)	1.840	30
Nearness to home operation	1.680	31
Nearness to operations in a "third country"	1.440	32

[a] n = 25.

TABLE 4-39

IMPORTANCE OF PLANT LOCATION FACTORS FOR SMALL EMPLOYEE-SIZE PLANTS, BY RANK ORDER OF MEAN RATINGS [a]

Factor	Mean Rating	Rank
Nearness to markets within the U.S.	3.798	1
Availability of transportation services	3.675	2
Ample space for future expansion	3.544	3
Availability of suitable plant sites	3.535	4
Labor attitudes	3.465	5
Availability of utilities	3.237	6
Cost of construction	3.149	7
Labor laws	3.123	8
Availability of skilled labor	3.070	9
Attitudes of local citizens	3.053	10
Cost of transportation services	3.044	11
Salary and wage rates	3.035	12
Cost of utilities	2.991	13
Local tax rates	2.956	14
State tax rates	2.930	15
Police and fire protection	2.930	15
Availability of managerial and technical personnel	2.886	17
Facilities for importing and exporting	2.868	18
Education facilities	2.860	19
Proximity to suppliers	2.772	20
Attitudes of government officials	2.737	21
Housing facilities	2.597	22
Proximity to raw material sources	2.456	23
Availability of unskilled labor	2.430	24
Cost of local capital	2.377	25
Government incentives	2.342	26
Availability of local capital	2.333	27
Climate	2.325	28
Cost of suitable land	2.290	29
Nearness to home operation	1.947	30
Proximity to export markets (outside the U.S.)	1.833	31
Nearness to operations in a "third country"	1.202	32

[a] n = 114.

TABLE 4-40

IMPORTANCE OF PLANT LOCATION FACTORS FOR MEDIUM EMPLOYEE-SIZE PLANTS, BY RANK ORDER OF MEAN RATINGS [a]

Factor	Mean Rating	Rank
Labor attitudes	3.973	1
Ample space for future expansion	3.918	2
Availability of transportation services	3.836	3
Availability of suitable plant sites	3.753	4
Availability of utilities	3.644	5
Nearness to markets within the U.S.	3.589	6
Attitudes of local citizens	3.589	6
Labor laws	3.466	8
Cost of construction	3.466	8
Cost of suitable land	3.425	10
Availability of unskilled labor	3.315	11
Cost of utilities	3.260	12
Availability of skilled labor	3.233	13
Salary and wage rates	3.206	14
Cost of local capital	3.164	15
State tax rates	3.151	16
Cost of transportation services	3.151	16
Attitudes of government officials	3.082	18
Education facilities	3.069	19
Housing facilities	3.027	20
Local tax rates	2.959	21
Police and fire protection	2.877	22
Availability of managerial and technical personnel	2.808	23
Proximity to raw material sources	2.726	24
Proximity to suppliers	2.712	25
Climate	2.507	26
Facilities for importing and exporting	2.480	27
Government incentives	2.247	28
Availability of local capital	2.082	29
Nearness to home operation	1.712	30
Proximity to export markets (outside the U.S.)	1.603	31
Nearness to operations in a "third country"	1.206	32

[a] $n = 73$.

TABLE 4-41

IMPORTANCE OF PLANT LOCATION FACTORS FOR LARGE
EMPLOYEE-SIZE PLANTS, BY RANK ORDER OF MEAN RATINGS [a]

Factor	Mean Rating	Rank
Labor attitudes	3.964	1
Availability of skilled labor	3.786	2
Availability of suitable plant sites	3.786	2
Attitudes of local citizens	3.786	2
Availability of transportation services	3.714	5
Ample space for future expansion	3.679	6
Availability of utilities	3.536	7
Government incentives	3.536	7
Cost of construction	3.500	9
Availability of managerial and technical personnel	3.500	9
Cost of utilities	3.464	11
Cost of suitable land	3.464	11
Attitudes of government officials	3.464	11
Cost of transportation services	3.429	14
Salary and wage rates	3.393	15
Nearness to markets within the U.S.	3.321	16
State tax rates	3.321	16
Labor laws	3.250	18
Availability of unskilled labor	3.214	19
Education facilities	3.107	20
Police and fire protection	2.929	21
Proximity to suppliers	2.857	22
Housing facilities	2.821	23
Proximity to raw material sources	2.643	24
Climate	2.393	25
Facilities for importing and exporting	2.357	26
Availabilityof local capital	2.321	27
Local tax rates	2.286	28
Cost of local capital	2.250	29
Proximity to export markets (outside the U.S.)	1.929	30
Nearness to home operation	1.571	31
Nearness to operations in a "third country"	1.393	32

[a] n = 28.

TABLE 4-42

IMPORTANCE OF PLANT LOCATION FACTORS FOR FIRMS WITH LOW DEGREE OF FOREIGN OWNERSHIP, BY RANK ORDER OF MEAN RATINGS [a]

Factor	Mean Rating	Rank
Labor attitudes	4.429	1
Cost of utilities	4.429	1
Labor laws	4.286	2
Availability of utilities	4.286	2
Availability of transportation services	4.286	2
Availability of suitable plant sites	4.000	6
State tax rates	3.857	7
Cost of construction	3.857	7
Salary and wage rates	3.857	7
Attitudes of government officials	3.857	7
Attitudes of local citizens	3.714	11
Local tax rates	3.714	11
Cost of transportation services	3.571	13
Nearness to markets within the U.S.	3.571	13
Ample space for future expansion	3.571	13
Cost of suitable land	3.571	13
Cost of local capital	3.571	13
Government incentives	3.429	18
Housing facilities	3.286	19
Education facilities	3.143	20
Police and fire protection	3.143	20
Climate	3.143	20
Facilities for importing and exporting	3.143	20
Availability of unskilled labor	3.000	24
Proximity to suppliers	3.000	24
Availability of local capital	2.857	26
Availability of managerial and technical personnel	2.714	27
Proximity to raw material sources	2.571	28
Availability of skilled labor	2.286	29
Nearness to home operation	2.000	30
Proximity to export markets (outside the U.S.)	1.857	31
Nearness to operations in a "third country"	1.143	32

[a] $n = 7$.

TABLE 4-43

IMPORTANCE OF PLANT LOCATION FACTORS FOR FIRMS WITH LOWER-MEDIUM DEGREE OF FOREIGN OWNERSHIP, BY RANK ORDER OF MEAN RATINGS [a]

Factor	Mean Rating	Rank
Labor attitudes	4.500	1
Ample space for future expansion	4.375	2
Proximity to suppliers	4.000	3
Salary and wage rates	4.000	3
Availability of transportation services	4.000	3
Availability of suitable plant sites	4.000	3
Labor laws	3.750	7
Availability of skilled labor	3.750	7
Availability of unskilled labor	3.625	9
Availability of managerial and technical personnel	3.625	9
Nearness to markets within the U.S.	3.500	11
Cost of transportation services	3.500	11
Proximity to raw material sources	3.375	13
Attitudes of local citizens	3.375	13
Education facilities	3.375	13
Cost of suitable land	3.375	13
Availability of utilities	3.250	17
Cost of construction	3.125	18
Housing facilities	3.125	18
Cost of utilities	3.000	20
Police and fire protection	2.875	21
State tax rates	2.875	21
Local tax rates	2.750	23
Attitudes of government officials	2.750	23
Nearness to home operation	2.625	25
Facilities for importing and exporting	2.500	26
Availability of local capital	2.375	27
Cost of local capital	2.250	28
Proximity to export markets (outside the U.S.)	2.250	28
Climate	2.250	28
Government incentives	1.625	31
Nearness to operations in a "third country"	1.250	32

[a] $n = 8$.

TABLE 4-44

IMPORTANCE OF PLANT LOCATION FACTORS FOR FIRMS WITH
UPPER-MEDIUM DEGREE OF FOREIGN OWNERSHIP, BY RANK ORDER
OF MEAN RATINGS [a]

Factor	Mean Rating	Rank
Availability of utilities	3.704	1
Nearness to markets within the U.S.	3.630	2
Availability of transportation services	3.630	2
Availability of suitable plant sites	3.630	2
Ample space for future expansion	3.556	5
Attitudes of local citizens	3.556	5
Labor attitudes	3.482	7
Cost of utilities	3.222	8
Cost of suitable land	3.222	8
Cost of construction	3.222	8
Labor laws	3.111	11
Availability of skilled labor	3.000	12
Attitudes of government officials	2.963	13
Availability of unskilled labor	2.963	13
Salary and wage rates	2.926	15
Police and fire protection	2.852	16
Local tax rates	2.852	16
Education facilities	2.815	18
Proximity to raw material sources	2.778	19
Cost of transportation services	2.778	19
State tax rates	2.741	21
Housing facilities	2.704	22
Availability of managerial and technical personnel	2.667	23
Proximity to suppliers	2.482	24
Cost of local capital	2.222	25
Government incentives	2.222	25
Availability of local capital	2.185	27
Facilities for importing and exporting	2.074	28
Climate	2.074	28
Proximity to export markets (outside the U.S.)	1.815	30
Nearness to home operation	1.667	31
Nearness to operations in a "third country"	1.074	32

[a] n = 27.

TABLE 4-45

IMPORTANCE OF PLANT LOCATION FACTORS FOR FIRMS WITH HIGH DEGREE OF FOREIGN OWNERSHIP BY RANK ORDER OF MEAN RATINGS [a]

Factor	Mean Rating	Rank
Nearness to markets within the U.S.	3.688	1
Availability of transportation services	3.688	1
Ample space for future expansion	3.671	3
Labor attitudes	3.625	4
Availability of suitable plant sites	3.563	5
Cost of suitable land	3.330	6
Availability of utilities	3.318	7
Cost of construction	3.273	8
Attitudes of local citizens	3.222	9
Availability of skilled labor	3.210	10
Labor laws	3.171	11
Cost of transportation services	3.119	12
Salary and wage rates	3.080	13
Cost of utilities	3.080	13
State tax rates	3.063	15
Local tax rates	2.989	16
Education facilities	2.949	17
Availability of managerial and technical personnel	2.938	18
Police and fire protection	2.875	19
Attitudes of government officials	2.869	20
Facilities for importing and exporting	2.744	21
Housing facilities	2.727	22
Availability of unskilled labor	2.722	23
Proximity to suppliers	2.716	24
Proximity to raw material sources	2.460	25
Climate	2.403	26
Government incentives	2.296	27
Cost of local capital	2.244	28
Availability of local capital	2.199	29
Nearness to home operation	1.790	30
Proximity to export markets (outside the U.S.)	1.727	31
Nearness to operations in a "third country"	1.222	32

[a] n = 176.

TABLE 4-46

ANOVA TEST RESULTS OF THE IMPORTANCE OF EACH PLANT LOCATION
FACTOR, BY PRODUCT CATEGORY

Factor	Obtained F [a]	Test Result [b]
Nearness to markets within the U.S.	0.88	NS
Proximity to export markets (outside the U.S.)	0.53	NS
Nearness to home operation	1.13	NS
Nearness to operations in a "third country"	0.81	NS
Facilities for importing and exporting	1.45	NS
Proximity to raw material sources	2.63	S
Proximity to suppliers	1.72	S
Availability of managerial and technical personnel	1.12	NS
Availability of skilled labor	1.63	S
Availability of unskilled labor	1.40	NS
Salary and wage rates	0.71	NS
Labor attitudes	0.58	NS
Labor laws	0.36	NS
Availability of utilities	1.09	NS
Cost of utilities	0.70	NS
Availability of transportation services	0.93	NS
Cost of transportation services	1.04	NS
Availability of suitable plant sites	1.24	NS
Cost of suitable land	1.18	NS
Cost of construction	1.07	NS
Ample space for future expansion	1.28	NS
Availability of local capital	1.56	NS
Cost of local capital	1.40	NS
State tax rates	0.69	NS
Local tax rates	0.72	NS
Government incentives	1.55	NS
Attitudes of government officials	0.78	NS
Attitudes of local citizens	0.79	NS
Housing facilities	0.73	NS
Education facilities	1.01	NS
Police and fire protection	0.52	NS
Climate	1.21	NS

[a] The associated degrees of freedom for between groups and within groups are 10 and 171, respectively.

[b] S = Significant; NS = Not significant.

TABLE 4-47

MEAN IMPORTANCE RATINGS OF FACTORS SHOWING SIGNIFICANT
HYPOTHESIS-TESTING RESULTS, BY PRODUCT CATEGORY

SIC	Product Category	Proximity to Raw Material Sources	Proximity to Suppliers	Availability of Skilled Labor
20	Food and kindred products	3.769	3.538	2.615
22	Textile mill products	2.643	2.714	3.071
26	Paper and related products	2.700	3.100	2.700
28	Chemicals and allied products	3.188	2.438	3.094
30	Rubber and plastics products	2.727	2.545	2.909
32	Stone, clay, glass, and concrete products	2.714	2.000	2.286
33	Primary metals	2.833	3.167	3.833
34	Fabricated metal products	2.111	2.444	3.472
35	Industrial machinery	2.167	2.900	3.400
36	Electrical machinery, equipment, and supplies	2.167	2.944	3.222
38	Measuring, analyzing, and control equipment	2.200	3.000	3.400
	Total	2.593	2.731	3.165

TABLE 4-48

ANOVA TEST RESULTS OF THE IMPORTANCE OF EACH PLANT
LOCATION FACTOR, BY PLANT SIZE

Factor	Obtained F [a]	Test Result [b]
Nearness to markets within the U.S.	1.99	NS
Proximity to export markets (outside the U.S.)	1.38	NS
Nearness to home operation	1.39	NS
Nearness to operations in a "third country"	0.90	NS
Facilities for importing and exporting	2.53	S
Proximity to raw material sources	0.90	NS
Proximity to suppliers	0.17	NS
Availability of managerial and technical personnel	3.65	S
Availability of skilled labor	4.72	S
Availability of unskilled labor	15.06	S
Salary and wage rates	1.31	NS
Labor attitudes	4.60	S
Labor laws	1.47	NS
Availability of utilities	2.55	S
Cost of utilities	2.60	S
Availability of transportation services	0.49	NS
Cost of transportation services	1.33	NS
Availability of suitable plant sites	0.94	NS
Cost of suitable land	0.44	NS
Cost of construction	2.23	NS
Ample space for future expansion	2.75	S
Availability of local capital	0.83	NS
Cost of local capital	0.57	NS
State tax rates	1.86	NS
Local tax rates	1.11	NS
Government incentives	0.51	NS
Attitudes of government officials	3.72	S
Attitudes of local citizens	6.37	S
Housing facilities	3.26	S
Education facilities	0.96	NS
Police and fire protection	0.06	NS
Climate	0.56	NS

[a] The associated degrees of freedom for between groups and within groups are 2 and 212, respectively.

[b] S = Significant; NS = Not significant.

TABLE 4-49

MEAN IMPORTANCE RATINGS OF FACTORS SHOWING SIGNIFICANT
HYPOTHESIS-TESTING RESULTS, BY PLANT SIZE

Factor	Plant Size			Total
	Small	Medium	Large	
Facilities for importing and exporting	2.868	2.479	2.357	2.670
Availability of managerial and technical personnel	2.886	2.808	3.500	2.940
Availability of skilled labor	3.070	3.233	3.786	3.219
Availability of unskilled labor	2.430	3.315	3.214	2.833
Labor attitudes	3.465	3.973	3.964	3.702
Availability of utilities	3.237	3.644	3.536	3.414
Cost of utilities	2.991	3.260	3.464	3.144
Ample space for future expansion	3.544	3.918	3.679	3.688
Attitudes of government officials	2.737	3.082	3.434	2.949
Attitudes of local citizens	3.053	3.589	3.786	3.330
Housing faciliites	2.596	3.027	2.821	2.772

TABLE 4-50

ANOVA TEST RESULTS OF THE IMPORTANCE OF EACH PLANT LOCATION FACTOR, BY STATE OF PLANT LOCATION

Factor	Obtained F [a]	Test Result [b]
Nearness to markets within the U.S.	1.58	S
Proximity to export markets (outside the U.S.)	1.09	NS
Nearness to home operation	4.27	S
Nearness to operations in a "third country"	1.08	NS
Facilities for importing and exporting	2.06	S
Proximity to raw material sources	2.14	S
Proximity to suppliers	1.91	S
Availability of managerial and technical personnel	0.92	NS
Availability of skilled labor	1.96	S
Availability of unskilled labor	1.33	NS
Salary and wage rates	2.00	S
Labor attitudes	1.38	NS
Labor laws	1.27	NS
Availability of utilities	1.67	S
Cost of utilities	1.08	NS
Availability of transportation services	2.03	S
Cost of transportation services	1.70	S
Availability of suitable plant sites	1.79	S
Cost of suitable land	1.82	S
Cost of construction	1.40	NS
Ample space for future expansion	1.14	NS
Availability of local capital	0.79	NS
Cost of local capital	0.61	NS
State tax rates	0.64	NS
Local tax rates	1.07	NS
Government incentives	2.12	S
Attitudes of government officials	1.89	S
Attitudes of local citizens	1.70	S
Housing facilities	1.34	NS
Education facilities	1.40	NS
Police and fire protection	1.11	NS
Climate	1.43	NS

[a] The associated degrees of freedom for between groups and within groups are 11 and 147, respectively.

[b] S = Significant; NS = Not significant.

TABLE 4-51

MEAN IMPORTANCE RATINGS OF FACTORS SHOWING SIGNIFICANT HYPOTHESIS-TESTING RESULTS, BY STATE OF PLANT LOCATION

Factor	Georgia	Illinois	Indiana	Massa-chusetts	New Jersey	New York	North Carolina	Ohio	Pennsyl-vania	South Carolina	Texas	Virginia	Total
Nearness to markets within the U.S.	4.000	3.200	4.143	3.200	3.333	3.500	3.333	4.333	3.667	4.300	3.286	3.400	3.673
Nearness to home operation	1.250	1.600	1.286	1.400	2.600	3.167	1.667	2.000	1.583	1.200	1.857	1.680	1.792
Facilities for importing and exporting	2.208	1.600	2.000	3.400	3.267	3.111	3.133	2.667	2.333	3.150	2.143	3.120	2.698
Proximity to raw material sources	2.708	1.600	2.286	1.000	2.267	2.167	1.867	3.000	2.000	2.500	3.429	1.920	2.258
Proximity to suppliers	2.750	2.800	2.429	2.000	3.133	2.444	2.267	4.000	2.500	2.900	2.857	2.320	2.654
Availability of skilled labor	3.083	2.800	2.429	2.800	3.400	2.889	3.467	4.500	3.417	3.500	3.714	3.000	3.226
Salary and wage rates	3.500	1.800	3.286	2.000	2.800	3.000	3.533	3.000	3.500	3.550	3.286	3.080	3.182
Availability of utilities	3.333	1.600	3.000	2.400	3.133	3.333	3.467	4.000	3.500	3.100	3.857	3.520	3.289
Availability of transportation services	3.875	2.200	3.286	2.800	3.733	3.722	3.533	4.667	3.667	3.600	4.286	3.840	3.692
Cost of transportation services	3.208	1.600	2.714	2.400	3.000	3.389	3.000	3.500	3.500	2.700	3.429	3.200	3.069
Availability of suitable plant sites	3.917	1.800	3.000	2.800	3.333	3.778	3.667	3.833	3.583	3.450	4.143	3.800	3.585
Cost of suitable land	3.458	2.200	3.000	1.800	3.200	3.333	3.733	3.667	3.500	3.600	4.000	3.480	3.390
Government incentives	2.292	1.200	2.000	2.000	1.667	3.056	2.133	1.667	3.000	2.300	1.714	2.360	2.264
Attitudes of government officials	2.917	1.200	3.143	2.000	2.400	3.278	3.333	2.000	3.333	3.000	3.143	2.920	2.893
Attitudes of local citizens	3.125	1.800	3.143	2.000	3.000	3.389	3.667	3.000	3.417	3.800	3.429	3.360	3.270

TABLE 4-52

ANOVA TEST RESULTS OF THE IMPORTANCE OF EACH PLANT LOCATION FACTOR, BY REGION OF PLANT LOCATION [a]

Factor	Obtained F [b]	Test Result [c]
Nearness to markets within the U.S.	1.09	NS
Proximity to export markets (outside the U.S.)	2.20	S
Nearness to home operation	4.36	S
Nearness to operations in a "third country"	0.50	NS
Facilities for importing and exporting	1.59	NS
Proximity to raw material sources	5.39	S
Proximity to suppliers	1.32	NS
Availability of managerial and technical personnel	1.10	NS
Availability of skilled labor	1.23	NS
Availability of unskilled labor	1.66	NS
Salary and wage rates	2.79	S
Labor attitudes	3.61	S
Labor laws	2.54	S
Availability of utilities	1.93	S
Cost of utilities	2.24	S
Availability of transportation services	2.16	S
Cost of transportation services	1.83	S
Availability of suitable plant sites	0.59	NS
Cost of suitable land	1.26	NS
Cost of construction	1.34	NS
Ample space for future expansion	0.63	NS
Availability of local capital	0.94	NS
Cost of local capital	0.73	NS
State tax rates	1.07	NS
Local tax rates	0.79	NS
Government incentives	1.35	NS
Attitudes of government officials	1.30	NS
Attitudes of local citizens	1.67	NS
Housing facilities	0.68	NS
Education facilities	1.08	NS
Police and fire protection	1.10	NS
Climate	1.78	S

[a] Since only three foreign manufacturers in the Mountain region responded, they were not included in tests of these hypotheses.

[b] The associated degrees of freedom for between groups and within groups are 7 and 213, respectively.

[c] S = Significant; NS = Not significant.

TABLE 4-53

MEAN IMPORTANCE RATINGS OF FACTORS SHOWING SIGNIFICANT HYPOTHESIS-TESTING RESULTS, BY REGION OF PLANT LOCATION

Factor	New England	Middle Atlantic	East North Central	West North Central	South Atlantic	East South Central	West South Central	Pacific	Total
Proximity to export markets (outside the U.S.)	1.273	1.711	1.565	1.667	1.722	2.083	1.692	2.750	1.751
Nearness to home operation	2.455	2.556	1.696	1.733	1.478	1.917	1.462	1.417	1.805
Proximity to raw material sources	1.818	2.156	2.478	3.533	2.300	2.833	3.615	3.583	2.525
Salary and wage rates	2.455	3.067	2.783	3.400	3.356	3.167	3.241	2.167	3.113
Labor attitudes	3.273	3.378	3.522	3.933	3.922	4.167	3.769	2.333	3.656
Labor laws	2.818	2.978	2.826	3.667	3.544	3.417	3.000	2.333	3.222
Availability of utilities	2.909	3.311	3.087	4.200	3.378	3.583	3.692	2.750	3.362
Cost of utilities	2.909	3.044	2.783	3.800	3.089	3.250	3.846	2.667	3.118
Availability of transportation services	3.364	3.711	3.391	4.333	3.744	3.333	4.231	3.167	3.697
Cost of transportation services	2.545	3.289	2.826	3.800	3.044	3.000	3.308	2.750	3.095
Climate	1.909	2.222	2.043	2.200	2.667	2.500	2.000	2.417	2.380

TABLE 4-54

ANOVA TEST RESULTS OF THE IMPORTANCE OF EACH PLANT LOCATION FACTOR, BY DEGREE OF FOREIGN OWNERSHIP

Factor	Obtained F [a]	Test Result [b]
Nearness to markets within the U.S.	0.09	NS
Proximity to export markets (outside the U.S.)	0.64	NS
Nearness to home operation	1.30	NS
Nearness to operations in a "third country"	0.44	NS
Facilities for importing and exporting	2.10	S
Proximity to raw material sources	1.48	NS
Proximity to suppliers	4.10	S
Availability of managerial and technical personnel	1.36	NS
Availability of skilled labor	0.91	NS
Availability of unskilled labor	1.66	NS
Salary and wage rates	2.95	S
Labor attitudes	2.32	S
Labor laws	2.03	NS
Availability of utilities	1.98	NS
Cost of utilities	3.29	S
Availability of transportation services	0.87	NS
Cost of transportation services	1.44	NS
Availability of suitable plant sites	0.57	NS
Cost of suitable land	0.17	NS
Cost of construction	0.63	NS
Ample space for future expansion	1.24	NS
Availability of local capital	0.57	NS
Cost of local capital	2.20	S
State tax rates	2.07	NS
Local tax rates	1.30	NS
Government incentives	2.65	S
Attitudes of government officials	1.19	NS
Attitudes of local citizens	0.81	NS
Housing facilities	0.81	NS
Education facilities	0.52	NS
Police and fire protection	0.14	NS
Climate	1.73	NS

[a] The associated degrees of freedom for between groups and within groups are 3 and 214, respectively.

[b] S = Significant; NS = Not significant.

TABLE 4-55
MEAN IMPORTANCE RATINGS OF FACTORS SHOWING SIGNIFICANT HYPOTHESIS-TESTING RESULTS, BY DEGREE OF FOREIGN OWNERSHIP

| Factor | Degree of Foreign Ownership | | | | |
	Low	Lower-Medium	Upper-Medium	High	Total
Facilities for importing and exporting	3.143	2.500	2.074	2.744	2.665
Proximity to suppliers	3.000	4.000	2.481	2.716	2.743
Salary and wage rates	3.857	4.000	2.926	3.080	3.119
Labor attitudes	4.429	4.500	3.481	3.625	3.665
Cost of utilities	4.429	3.000	3.222	3.080	3.183
Cost of local capital	3.571	2.250	2.222	2.244	2.284
Government incentives	3.429	1.625	2.222	2.295	2.298

TABLE 4-56

ANOVA TEST RESULTS OF THE IMPORTANCE OF EACH PLANT LOCATION FACTOR, BY NATIONALITY OF OWNERSHIP

Factor	Obtained F [a]	Test Result [b]
Nearness to markets within the U.S.	0.17	NS
Proximity to export markets (outside the U.S.)	1.56	NS
Nearness to home operation	3.68	S
Nearness to operations in a "third country"	2.26	S
Facilities for importing and exporting	0.32	NS
Proximity to raw material sources	2.13	S
Proximity to suppliers	0.33	NS
Availability of managerial and technical personnel	1.31	NS
Availability of skilled labor	0.87	NS
Availability of unskilled labor	1.47	NS
Salary and wage rates	2.35	S
Labor attitudes	1.62	NS
Labor laws	1.28	NS
Availability of utilities	1.01	NS
Cost of utilities	0.67	NS
Availability of transportation services	0.83	NS
Cost of transportation services	1.05	NS
Availability of suitable plant sites	1.29	NS
Cost of suitable land	1.12	NS
Cost of construction	0.62	NS
Ample space for future expansion	0.97	NS
Availability of local capital	0.70	NS
Cost of local capital	0.86	NS
State tax rates	0.56	NS
Local tax rates	0.82	NS
Government incentives	0.44	NS
Attitudes of government officials	1.57	NS
Attitudes of local citizens	1.91	NS
Housing facilities	1.25	NS
Education facilities	1.88	NS
Police and fire protection	2.13	S
Climate	2.61	S

[a] The associated degrees of freedom for between groups and within groups are 7 and 197, respectively.

[b] S = Significant; NS = Not significant.

TABLE 4-57

MEAN IMPORTANCE RATINGS OF FACTORS SHOWING SIGNIFICANT HYPOTHESIS-TESTING RESULTS, BY NATIONALITY OF OWNERSHIP

Factor	Canada	France	Germany	Japan	Netherlands	Sweden	Switzerland	United Kingdom	Total
Nearness to home operation	2.800	1.714	1.679	1.393	1.200	2.200	1.824	1.732	1.844
Nearness to operations in a "third country"	1.200	1.095	1.302	1.179	1.000	2.000	1.059	1.171	1.229
Proximity to raw material sources	2.933	2.476	2.340	3.071	3.400	2.300	2.824	2.122	2.561
Salary and wage rates	3.000	2.810	3.453	3.393	2.400	2.400	2.706	3.171	3.117
Police and fire protection	2.900	2.143	3.057	3.107	2.400	2.600	3.059	2.902	2.878
Climate	1.967	1.810	2.642	2.821	2.200	2.500	2.647	2.244	2.385

TABLE 4-58
FACTOR ANALYSIS OF PLANT LOCATION FACTORS

Plant Location Factor	Dimension								Communality
	1	2	3	4	5	6	7	8	
Nearness to markets within the U.S.	-0.03179	0.01237	0.03748	0.09641	0.33933	0.01644	0.08451	-0.13292	0.15209
Proximity to export markets (outside the U.S.)	-0.03646	0.12753	0.07788	0.26906	0.31337	0.03503	0.06684	0.31669	0.30024
Nearness to home operation	-0.01238	0.00547	0.07344	0.12974	-0.17974	0.14203	-0.08720	0.31844	0.15342
Nearness to operations in a "third country"	-0.07074	0.05068	0.02861	-0.02012	0.04979	-0.01601	0.02234	0.42894	0.19602
Facilities for importing & exporting	-0.08014	-0.01914	0.15201	0.27696	0.13564	0.00224	0.11272	0.50431	0.39204
Proximity to raw material sources	0.12727	-0.01487	0.07658	0.04622	0.59896	-0.00188	-0.02460	0.13277	0.40141
Proximity to suppliers	0.12653	0.12660	0.01931	0.09043	0.65252	0.44097	0.02927	0.14104	0.68158
Availability of managerial & technical personnel	0.11020	0.03124	0.04208	0.19256	0.14477	0.70093	0.12052	0.00338	0.57877
Availability of skilled labor	0.26234	-0.00550	0.16035	0.11552	0.03081	0.58821	0.04989	0.08949	0.46535
Availability of unskilled labor	0.48331	0.12114	0.24030	0.10006	0.02829	0.08003	0.01724	0.18633	0.35824
Salary and wage rates	0.59897	0.14643	0.22202	0.06307	-0.00991	0.20995	0.07764	0.00211	0.48369
Labor attitudes	0.64126	0.00276	0.32239	0.21255	-0.05880	0.31045	0.17530	0.06834	0.69557
Labor laws	0.62346	0.05266	0.19146	0.17595	0.08217	0.27344	0.22325	0.00979	0.59056
Availability of utilities	0.46810	-0.08861	0.43805	0.23812	0.23351	0.01211	0.31149	-0.15913	0.65259
Cost of utilities	0.47391	0.02316	0.38401	0.24545	0.22031	0.00219	0.36892	-0.11186	0.63000
Availability of transportation services	0.21614	-0.05000	0.51202	0.09575	0.33672	0.03737	0.24300	0.16144	0.51381
Cost of transportation services	0.31401	0.07682	0.44414	0.07830	0.32211	0.08456	0.36185	0.05272	0.55252
Availability of suitable plant sites	0.20889	0.00336	0.73274	0.19423	0.03984	0.08115	0.05367	0.19726	0.66825
Cost of suitable land	0.14338	0.25093	0.68546	0.17431	-0.00175	0.01480	0.10773	0.11820	0.60957
Cost of construction	0.23105	0.22042	0.55203	0.31452	-0.00376	0.08809	0.09835	0.03619	0.52439
Ample space for future expansion	0.27484	0.08704	0.61170	0.22414	0.05662	0.18150	0.00240	0.02437	0.54673
Availability of local capital	0.08037	0.88725	0.13310	0.06180	0.00955	0.04448	0.11121	0.04955	0.83210
Cost of local capital	0.11767	0.90450	0.15246	0.05144	0.06727	0.01138	0.15023	0.04482	0.88709
State tax rates	0.30371	0.31206	0.18574	0.22092	0.07253	0.17564	0.71325	0.03233	0.81881
Local tax rates	0.32940	0.26522	0.21506	0.22849	0.06976	0.13790	0.74515	0.05365	0.85932
Government incentives	0.45473	0.36557	-0.07095	0.05524	0.11866	-0.05200	0.25157	0.30241	0.52003
Attitudes of government officials	0.66489	0.07228	0.13286	0.27660	0.11901	0.00285	0.18806	0.24712	0.65207
Attitudes of local citizens	0.65218	0.00462	0.23800	0.45189	0.11190	0.02591	0.04322	0.06715	0.70578
Housing facilities	0.26241	0.07983	0.17259	0.80710	0.12574	0.09152	0.07993	-0.00299	0.78578
Education facilities	0.23038	0.00498	0.23649	0.84553	0.08512	0.14902	0.05537	0.02874	0.85729
Police and fire protection	0.25447	0.05259	0.31692	0.62315	0.17609	0.11671	0.11675	0.03787	0.61598
Climate	0.12842	0.05199	0.13099	0.47875	0.06350	0.12482	0.18442	0.06572	0.32351
EIGENVALUE	9.83126	1.97029	1.39511	1.27210	1.11204	0.94233	0.80559	0.67726	

TABLE 4-59

RELATIONSHIPS BETWEEN DIMENSIONS AND PLANT LOCATION
FACTORS

Dimension	Plant Location Factor	Factor Loading
1. Attitudes of people, labor conditions, and utilities	Attitudes of government officials	0.66489
	Attitudes of local citizens	0.65218
	Labor attitudes	0.64126
	Labor laws	0.62346
	Salary and wages	0.59897
	Availability of unskilled labor	0.48331
	Cost of utilities	0.47391
	Availability of utilities	0.46810
	Government incentives	0.45473
2. Local capital	Cost of local capital	0.90450
	Availability of local capital	0.88725
3. Suitable land and transportation services	Availability of suitable plant sites	0.73274
	Cost of suitable land	0.68546
	Ample space for future expansion	0.61370
	Cost of construction	0.55203
	Availability of transportation services	0.51202
	Cost of transportation services	0.44414
4. Community environment	Education facilities	0.84553
	Housing facilities	0.80710
	Police and fire protection	0.62315
	Climate	0.47875
5. Nearness to supply sources and markets	Proximity to suppliers	0.65252
	Proximity to raw material sources	0.59896
	Nearness to markets within the U.S.	0.33933
6. Availability of managerial personnel and skilled labor	Availability of managerial and technical personnel	0.70093
	Availability of skilled labor	0.58821
7. Tax rates	Local tax rates	0.74515
	State tax rates	0.71324
8. Import-export considerations	Facilities for importing and exporting	0.50431
	Nearness to operations in a "third country"	0.42894
	Nearness to home operation	0.31844
	Proximity to export markets (outside the U.S.)	0.31669

TABLE 4-60

COMMUNICATION SOURCES USED BY FOREIGN MANUFACTURING
INVESTORS TO DECIDE IN WHICH U.S. COMMUNITY TO LOCATE
THEIR PLANT

	Number	Percent
State agencies	111	25.1
Local agencies	96	21.7
Other firms	67	15.1
Outside consultant	51	11.5
U.S. Department of Commerce	33	7.5
Investment missions	26	5.9
Company staffs' knowledge, research, and experience	17	3.8
Owner's personal experience	12	2.8
Local chamber of commerce	8	1.8
U.S. customers	6	1.4
Local investors	4	0.9
Local real estate	3	0.7
Utility company	2	0.5
Foreign Government's trade department	2	0.5
Local banks	1	0.2
Railroad company	1	0.2
Attorney	1	0.2
U.S. Department of Agriculture	1	0.2
Total	442 [a]	100.0

[a] Because the respondents were asked to check all the information sources they used, this number exceeds 224.

CHAPTER V

SUMMARY, CONCLUSIONS, IMPLICATIONS, AND RECOMMENDATIONS

This chapter starts out with a summary of the research objectives, problems, and methodology. Conclusions are then drawn based on the empirical findings. Following that is a discussion of what is hinted at or suggested, but not plainly expressed in the results of the data analysis. Finally, some topics for further research are recommended.

SUMMARY OF THE RESEARCH

The establishment of foreign manufacturing plants in the U.S. assists the economic development of the U.S. in at least four important ways:
1. It increases the national employment level.
2. It helps balance the U.S. international payments.
3. It reduces the inflationary pressure.
4. It induces the transfer of technology from abroad.

Thus research that could help lure more foreign manufacturing investors to this country should be welcome and valuable.

There were three primary objectives of this study: (1) to identify the factors which have important influence on non-American manufacturing investors in making locational choices for their plants in the U.S.; (2) to supply useful information to communities in the U.S. for improving their investment climates; and (3) to facilitate the exchange of opinions and experiences of choosing plant locations among foreign manufacturing investors in the U.S.

To achieve the above objectives, four specific problems were formulated:
1. What is the importance of various plant location factors in the eyes of foreign manufacturing investors in the U.S.?
2. What are the basic "dimensions" or "groupings" underlying this relatively large number of plant location factors?
3. From what sources do foreign manufacturing investors in the U.S. get information in order to decide in which community to locate their plant?
4. What percentage and what kinds of foreign manufacturers in the U.S. have not made a plant location decision and why?

Five sets of hypotheses were further designed to be statistically tested. The details concerning hypotheses are discussed in the next section.

A thorough literature review, including both theoretical works and empirical studies, provided a list of 32 plant location factors which might have influenced foreign manufacturing investors' plant location decisions in the U.S. These 32 plant location factors constituted part of the questionnaire used in this study. A mail survey was conducted. All together, 1147 foreign manufacturers in the U.S. were sent the questionnaire, and 254, or 22 percent, of them supplied usable information. The returned data were processed by the computer. Descriptive statistics were computed, factor analyses performed, and hypotheses tested.

CONCLUSIONS

Conclusions of hypotheses testing

First of all, the five hypothesis sets are repeated below:

Hypothesis set 1: The importance of a plant location factor varies by category of products produced by foreign manufacturers in the U.S.

Hypothesis set 2: The importance of a plant location factor varies by employee size of foreign manufacturing plants in the U.S.

Hypothesis set 3: The importance of a plant location factor varies by location within the U.S. of the foreign manufacturing plants.

Hypothesis set 4: The importance of a plant location factor varies by degree of foreign ownership in manufacturing firms in the U.S.

Hypothesis set 5: The importance of a plant location factor varies by national origin of foreign manufacturing investors in the U.S.

The results of hypothesis testings are summarized in Table 5-1. For hypothesis set 1, it is concluded that foreign manufacturers producing different categories of products weigh each of the following three plant location factors significantly differently: (1) proximity to raw material sources; (2) proximity to suppliers; and (3) availability of skilled labor. Mean importance ratings of these three factors, classified by product category, further indicate that:

1. The factor "proximity to raw material sources" is especially important to foreign manufacturers producing foods and kindred products, chemical and allied products, and primary metals.

2. The factor "proximity to suppliers" has special influence on foreign manufacturers producing food and kindred products, paper and related products, primary metals, and electrical machinery, equipment, and supplies.

3. The factor "availability of skilled labor" is considered particularly vital by foreign manufacturers in primary metal, fabricated metal, industrial machinery, and measuring-analyzing-control equipment industries.

Hypothesis set 2 was rejected for the following 11 factors: (1) facilities for importing and exporting; (2) availability of managerial and technical personnel; (3) availability of skilled labor; (4) availability of unskilled labor;

TABLE 5-1

SUMMARY OF HYPOTHESES-TESTING RESULTS [a]

Factor	Hypothesis Set					
	1	2	3A [b]	3B [b]	4	5
1. Nearness to markets within the U.S.			S [c]			
2. Proximity to export markets (outside the U.S.)				S		
3. Nearness to home operation			S	S		S
4. Nearness to operations in a "third country"						S
5. Facilities for importing and exporting		S	S		S	
6. Proximity to raw material sources	S	S	S	S		S
7. Proximity to suppliers	S		S		S	
8. Availability of managerial and technical personnel		S				
9. Availability of skilled labor	S	S	S			
10. Availability of unskilled labor		S				
11. Salary and wage rates			S	S	S	S
12. Labor attitudes		S		S	S	
13. Labor laws				S		
14. Availability of utilities		S	S	S		
15. Cost of utilities		S		S	S	
16. Availability of transportation services			S	S		
17. Cost of transportation services			S	S		
18. Availability of suitable plant sites			S			
19. Cost of suitable land			S			
20. Cost of construction						
21. Ample space for future expansion		S				
22. Availability of local capital						
23. Cost of local capital					S	
24. State tax rate						
25. Local tax rate						
26. Government incentives			S		S	
27. Attitudes of government officials		S	S			
28. Attitudes of local citizens		S	S			
29. Housing facilities		S				
30. Education facilities						
31. Police and fire protection						S
32. Climate				S		

[a] Only the significant results are indicated in the table.

[b] Hypothesis set 3 was tested at both the state (3A) and the regional (3B) level.

[c] S = Significant.

(5) labor attitudes; (6) availability of utilities; (7) cost of utilities; (8) ample space for future expansion; (9) attitudes of government officials; (10) attitudes of local citizens; and (11) housing facilities. This means that the importance of each of these 11 factors varies by employee size of foreign manufacturing plants. The relevant factor mean ratings further disclose that:

1. The factor "facilities for importing and exporting" is particularly important to small employee-size foreign manufacturing plants.
2. "Ample space for future expansion" and "housing facilities" are the two factors which are of special concern to the medium employee-size foreign plants.
3. Factors including "availability of managerial and technical personnel," "availability of skilled labor," "cost of utilities" and "attitudes of government officials" draw exceptionally high attention from large-size foreign manufacturing plants.
4. "Availability of unskilled labor," "labor attitudes," "availability of utilities," and "attitudes of local citizens" are the five factors which are considered more influential by medium and large employee-size foreign manufacturing plants than by small ones.

Hypothesis set 3 was tested at both the state and the regional level. At the state level, it is concluded that foreign manufacturers in different states weigh each of the following 15 factors significantly differently: (1) nearness to markets within the U.S.; (2) nearness to home operation; (3) facilities for importing and exporting; (4) proximity to raw material sources; (5) proximity to suppliers; (6) availability of skilled labor; (7) salary and wage rates; (8) availability of utilities; (9) availability of transportation services; (10) cost of transportation services; (11) availability of suitable plant sites; (12) cost of suitable land; (13) government incentives; (14) attitudes of government officials; and (15) attitudes of local citizens. Furthermore, mean importance ratings of these 15 factors, classified by state of plant location, reveal that:

1. The factor "nearness to markets within the U.S." is considered exceptionally important by foreign manufacturers in Georgia, Indiana, Ohio, and South Carolina.
2. The factor "nearness to home operation" has special importance to foreign manufacturers in New Jersey, New York, and Ohio.
3. The factor "facilities for importing and exporting" is of particular concern to foreign manufacturing investors in Massachusetts, New Jersey, New York, North Carolina, South Carolina, and Virginia.
4. "Proximity to raw material sources" is especially influential to foreign manufacturers in Georgia, Ohio, South Carolina, and Texas.
5. The factor "proximity to suppliers" draws extra attention of foreign manufacturers in New Jersey, Ohio, South Carolina, and Texas.

6. "Availability of skilled labor" is considered exceptionally important by foreign manufacturers in New Jersey, North Carolina, Ohio, South Carolina, and Texas.

7. The factor "salary and wage rates" has special importance to foreign manufacturers in Georgia, North Carolina, Pennsylvania, and South Carolina.

8. "Availability of utilities" is of particular concern to foreign manufacturing investors in Ohio, Pennsylvania, Texas, and Virginia.

9. The factor "availability of transportation services" is especially influential to foreign manufacturers in Ohio and Texas.

10. "Cost of transportation services" draws extra attention of foreign manufacturers in New York, Ohio, Pennsylvania, and Texas.

11. The factor "availability of suitable plant sites" is considered exceptionally important by foreign manufacturers in Georgia, Ohio, Texas, and Virginia.

12. "Cost of suitable land" has special importance to foreign manufacturers in North Carolina, Ohio, South Carolina, and Texas.

13. The factor "government incentives" is of particular concern to foreign manufacturing investors in New York and Pennsylvania.

14. The factor "attitudes of government officials" is especially influential to foreign manufacturers in Indiana, New York, North Carolina, Pennsylvania, and Texas.

15. The factor "attitudes of local citizens" draws extra attention of foreign manufacturers in North Carolina and South Carolina.

Hypothesis set 3 was rejected at the regional level for the following 11 factors: (1) proximity to export markets (outside the U.S.); (2) nearness to home operation; (3) proximity to raw material sources; (4) salary and wage rates; (5) labor attitudes; (6) labor laws; (7) availability of utilities; (8) cost of utilities; (9) availability of transportation services; (10) cost of transportation services; and (11) climate. This means that the importance of each of these eleven factors varies by region of foreign manufacturing plants. The relevant factor mean ratings further disclose that:

1. The factor "proximity to export markets (outside the U.S.)" is considered exceptionally important by foreign manufacturers in East South Central and Pacific regions.

2. "Nearness to home operation" has special importance to foreign manufacturers in New England and Middle Atlantic regions.

3. The factor "proximity to raw material sources" is of particular concern to foreign manufacturing investors in West North Central, East South Central, West South Central, and Pacific regions.

4. "Salary and wage rates" are especially influential to foreign manufacturers in West North Central and South Atlantic regions.

5. The factor "labor attitudes" draws unusual attention of foreign manufacturers in West North Central, South Atlantic, and East South Central regions.

6. "Labor laws" are considered exceptionally important by foreign manufacturers in West North Central and South Atlantic regions.

7. The factor "availability of utilities" has special importance to foreign manufacturers in West North Central, East South Central, and West South Central regions.

8. "Cost of utilities," "availability of transportation services," and "cost of transportation services" are of particular concern to foreign manufacturing investors in West North Central and West South Central regions.

9. The factor "climate" draws unusual attention of foreign manufacturers in South Atlantic region.

For hypothesis set 4, it is concluded that manufacturing firms with different degrees of foreign ownership weigh each of the following seven factors significantly differently: (1) facilities for importing and exporting; (2) proximity to suppliers; (3) salary and wage rates; (4) labor attitudes; (5) cost of utilities; (6) cost of local capital; and (7) government incentives. Mean importance ratings of these seven factors, classified by degree of foreign ownership, further indicate that:

1. Factors including "facilities for importing and exporting," "cost of utilities," "cost of local capital," and "government incentives" are especially important to manufacturing firms with low degree of foreign ownership.

2. "Proximity to suppliers," "salary and wage rates," and "labor attitudes" are considered particularly vital by manufacturing firms with low and lower-medium degree of foreign ownership.

Hypothesis set 5 was rejected for the following six factors: (1) nearness to home operation; (2) nearness to operations in a "third country"; (3) proximity to raw material sources; (4) salary and wage rates; (5) police and fire protection; and (6) climate. This means that the importance of each of these six factors varies by nationality of foreign manufacturing investors. The relevant factor mean ratings further reveal that:

1. The factor "nearness to home operation" is considered exceptionally important by Canadian and Swedish manufacturing investors.

2. "Nearness to operations" in a 'third country' " has special importance to Swedish manufacturers.

3. The factor "proximity to raw material sources" is of particular concern to Canadian, Japanese, Dutch, and Swiss manufacturing investors.

4. "Salary and wage rates" are especially influential to German and Japanese manufacturers.

5. The factor "police and fire protection" draws unusual attention of Japanese manufacturing investors.

6. "Climate" is considered exceptionally important by German, Japanese, and Swiss manufacturers.

General conclusions

Based on the empirical findings, slightly over half (53 percent) of the responding foreign manufacturing plants in the U.S. were designed to have 99 or less employees. One third (34 percent) of the responding firms reported that they had a planned employee size between 100 and 499 for their plant. The remaining 13 percent indicated an intended plant employee size of 500 or more.

In most (93 percent) of the foreign manufacturing firms in the U.S., non-Americans have 50 percent or more ownership. This conclusion, to some extent, supports Arpan's statement ". . . the initial funds for the (foreign manufacturing) investments came overwhelmingly from foreign parents. . ."[1]

Using mean importance rating as the evaluation criterion, the five most important plant location factors in the eyes of foreign manufacturing investors in the U.S. are: (1) availability of transportation services; (2) labor attitudes; (3) ample space for future expansion; (4) nearness to markets within the U.S.; and (5) availability of suitable plant sites.

Foster, in his article "The Friendly Invasion," stated, ". . . a major influence on almost all site locations by foreign-owned companies has to be the incentives offered by vaious states and regional development groups."[2] The results of this study do not seem to support this statement. The factor "government incentives" ranks only number 27 in the 32 plant-location-factor list.

The factor analysis of the survey data suggests that there are eight dimensions underlying the 32 plant location factors. On this basis, it is evident that plant location decisions of foreign manufacturing investors in the U.S. are most strongly affected by attitudes of American people, labor conditions, and utilities, to a much lesser extent by local capital, suitable land and transportation services, community environment, nearness to supply sources and markets, availability of managerial personnel and skilled labor, tax rates, and import-export considerations. This factor-analysis result is valuable because it summarizes the information of 32 plant location factors in 8 basic dimensions which are easier to grasp. Since factors within each dimension are essentially indicators of the same aspect of a plant location decision, 8 plant location factors, rather than 32, can be used in further research on this subject.

In order to decide in which community to locate their plant, foreign manufacturing investors obtain their information from: (1) state agencies (25 percent), (2) local agencies (22 percent), (3) other firms (15 percent),

(4) outside consultants (12 percent), (5) U.S. Department of Commerce (8 percent), (6) investment missions (6 percent), and (7) other sources (12 percent).

Twelve percent of the foreign manufacturers in the U.S. have never made a plant location decision in the U.S., but they do have a plant. This situation could happen because some foreign manufacturing investors bought an existing firm which owned a plant, while some others leased U.S. plants.

IMPLICATIONS

Implications for U.S. communities

The importance of plant location factors in the eyes of foreign manufacturing investors in the U.S. was investigated in this study. The findings can be used by U.S. communities as a valuable information input in programming their economic development plan. The community investment climate can be analyzed in light of the importance of various plant location factors. Both the strengths and the weaknesses of the community should be identified. The strengths can be emphasized in the process of luring foreign manufacturing investors, and the weaknesses need to be improved or eliminated if possible.

Based on the findings reported in this study and the local human and natural environmental conditions, the economic developers in the U.S. communities could get a basic idea about the characteristics, such as national origin, standard industrial classification, and plant employee size, of their most prospective foreign manufacturing investors. A program developed to lure foreign manufacturing investment based on this knowledge can be expected to produce more fruitful results.

The empirical findings in this study can also be used by U.S. economic developers in dealing with individual foreign-manufacturing-investment cases. For example, assume a German industrial-machinery manufacturer is requesting plant-location-decision information from a state economic development agency for its U.S. manufacturing investment, which will be wholly owned by the German parent firm and will have about 500 employees. In reference to Tables 4-10, 4-24, 4-41, and 4-45, the state development agency immediately knows that the following eight factors may need to be especially emphasized: labor attitudes, ample space for future expansion, nearness to markets within the U.S., availability of suitable plant sites, attitudes of local citizens, availability of transportation services, cost of suitable land, and availability of skilled labor.

Various communication sources used by foreign manufacturing investors were identified in the research. This information can be used to increase the effectiveness of disseminating relevant materials to foreign investment prospects.

The fact that "other firms" are used by many foreign manufacturing investors as communication sources signifies the importance of word-of-mouth information flow. On this point, the reputation or image of a community needs to be managed.

From the standpoint of promoting a community, those plant location factors showing significant hypothesis-testing results deserve special attention. This is because the factors are perceived as having different importance or values by different groups of foreign manufacturing investors. Referring to Table 5-1, the more significant results a plant location factor shows, the more emphasis it warrants.

Implications for present and potential foreign manufacturing investors in the U.S.

In this study, a list of 32 plant location factors was developed. Seventeen other relevant factors were further enumerated by the respondents, as presented in Chapter IV. Both the present and the potential foreign manufacturing investors in the U.S. can use these 49 factors as a check list to make sure that all the important aspects of the plant location decision have been taken into consideration.

A foreign manufacturing investor would make a better plant location decision in the U.S. if he or she has a fundamental knowledge about the importance of various plant location factors. Although it is true that each plant location decision is unique in its own way, generalizations are definitely valuable because, to a certain extent, they are relevant to any decisions. As an example, when a British firm is planning to build a small textile production plant in the U.S., the information in Tables 4-15, 4-17, and 4-39 indicates that the following eight factors may deserve special considerations: labor attitudes, availability of transportation services, ample space for future expansion, availability of suitable plant sites, availability of utilities, nearness to markets within the U.S., attitudes of local citizens, and labor laws.

To make a decision, especially a complex and important one, relevant information is certainly vital. Most, if not all, foreign manufacturing investors in the U.S. might have asked such a question at one time or another: where can we get information for making a plant location decision in the U.S.? The answer is provided in Chapter IV of this study, where 18 communication sources were reported. This is at least a very good starting point.

Implications for educators and researchers

As pointed out in Chapters I and II, at the present time there is a lack of empirical data on foreign manufacturing investors' activites in general and their plant-location-decision behaviors in particular. This research aims for filling a knowledge gap in this area. It is the first study which provides massive, solid empirical information on plant location decisions of foreign manufacturing investors in the U.S. In addition to the descriptive findings, the relationships between the importance of each plant location factor and five major characteristics of foreign manufacturing investors were statistically tested. Furthermore, the underlying dimensions of plant location factors were identified by use of a factor analysis. Educators and researchers in the fields of international marketing, logistics, economics, and geography should find this study valuable.

SUGGESTIONS FOR FURTHER RESEARCH

The empirical questioning of this study had its focus on communities rather than on regions or specific plant sites. This was because the major purpose of this reserach was to provide useful information to U.S. communities for improving their investment climate. It seems very obvious that similar studies can be, and probably should be, also conducted at the regional and plant site level.

Comparative research is needed concerning the plant location decisions between the U.S. domestic manufacturing investors and the foreign manufacturing investors. The finding of such a research could further assist U.S. communities in their economic development planning process.

This study examined the plant location decisions of foreign manufacturing investors in the U.S. Further research may be directed toward the investigation of their office and warehouse location decisions, logistical practices, promotional activities, pricing policies, marketing research efforts, and distribution channel designs.

In Chapter I, a conceptual plant-location-decision model was developed to show the focus of this study. If this model can be proved to be highly accurate and generalizable, then the economic developers can use it as a tool to detect which stage their foreign-manufacturing-investment prospect is in, and act accordingly, appropriately, and effectively.

NOTES

CHAPTER I

1. Herbert E. Dougall, *Investments,* 9th ed. (Englewood Cliffs, N.J.: Prentice-Hall, Inc., 1973), p. 1; Peter Davies, ed., *The American Heritage Dictionary* (New York: Dell Publishing Co., Inc., 1970), p. 374; C.L. Barnhart, ed., *The American College Dictionary* (New York: Random House, 1964), p. 642.

2. A detailed discussion about foreign investment is presented in Chapter II.

3. To be simple, the term "foreign manufacturing investment" will substitute for "inward foreign manufacturing investment" in the rest of this book.

4. U.S., Congress, House, *International Investment Uncertainty.* 94th Cong., 2nd sess. (Washington, D.C.: U.S. Government Printing Office, 1977), p. 18.

5. Ibid., p. 25.

6. Walter E. Greene, *Plant Location Factors* (Chicago: Adams Press, 1969), pp. 3-4.

7. U.S., Congress, House, *International Investment Uncertainty,* p. 25.

8. See for example, Joseph A. Russell, *Plant Location* (New York: American Research Council, Inc., 1956), p. v and vi; Sten Soderman, *Industrial Location Planning* (Stockholm: Almqvist and Wiksell International, 1975), p. 5; William B. Speir, "The Common Denominator in Selecting New Sites," *Industrial Development and Manufacturers Record* 138 (January/February 1969): 30.

9. F.E. LeVan, "Hardboiled Economics Guide DuPont in the Selection of Sites for Plants," *Industrial Development,* December, 1959, p. 6.

10. An operational definition of foreign manufacturing investors used in this study can be found in Chapter III.

11. U.S., Congress, House, *International Investment Uncertainty,* p. 18

12. See Chapter II.

13. William F. Massy, "Applying Factor Analysis to a Specific Marketing Problem," *Proceedings of the American Marketing Association Conference,* 1964, pp. 291-307; William D. Wells and Jagdish N. Sheth, "Factor Analysis in Marketing Research," in *Handbook of Market Research,* ed. Robert Ferber (New York: McGraw-Hill Book Company, 1971); Frederick Williams, *Reasoning with Statistics* (New York: Holt, Rinehart and Winston, Inc., 1968), pp. 151-66.

14. Jean Stoetzel, "A Factor Analysis of the Liquor Preferences of French Consumers," *Journal of Advertising Research* 1 (December 1960):7.

15. Frederick Williams, *Reasoning with Statistics,* p. 153.

16. The mathematical procedure used here was factor analysis.

17. John D. Daniels, *Recent Foreign Direct Manufacturing Investment in the United States* (New York: Praeger Publishers, Inc., 1971), pp. 64-65; Jeffrey S. Arpan and David

A. Ricks, *Directory of Foreign Manufacturers in the United States* (Atlanta: School of Business Administration, Georgia State University, 1975), p. xiv.

18. Simon Webley, *Foreign Direct Investment in the United States: Opportunities and Impediments* (London: British-North American Committee, 1974), p. 3; U.S., Congress, House, *International Investment Uncertainty,* p. 17.

19. Arpan, et al., *Directory of Foreign Manufacturers in the United States,* p. xvi.

20. Webley, *Foreign Direct Investment in the United States: Opportunities and Impediments,* p. 7.

21. Tom Foster, "The Friendly Invasion," *Distribution Worldwide* 75(December 1976):27.

22. See Appendix A-1 for a sample of the inquiry letter used.

23. Philip Kotler, *Marketing Management,* 2nd ed. (Englewood Cliffs, N.J.: Prentice-Hall, Inc., 1972), pp. 335-50.

24. William J. Stanton, *Fundamentals of Marketing,* 3rd ed. (New York: McGraw-Hill Book Company, 1971), pp. 36-39, 137-43; Richard D. Robinson, *International Business Management* (Hinsdale, Ill.: Dryden Press, 1973), pp. 15-24; Donald J. Bowersox, *Logistical Management* (New York: Macmillan Publishing Co., Inc., 1974), pp. 494-99.

25. "Japanese Firm Will Build Plant in U.S., Make Color TV Sets," *Lincoln Evening Journal,* 1 April 1977, p. 1.

26. Foster, "The Friendly Invasion," p. 28.

27. Ibid., p. 29.

28. Ronald H. Hermone, "The Data You Need to Select a Plant Site," *Management Review* 59 (November 1970):35-36.

29. Foster, "The Friendly Invasion," p. 28.

30. Hermone, "The Data You Need to Select a Plant Site," p. 36.

31. Bowersox, *Logistical Management,* p. 495.

32. Hermone, "The Data You Need to Select a Plant Site," p. 36.

33. Fredric Good, ed., *Plant Location* (New York: Simmons-Boardman Publishing Corp., 1975); Linca L. Liston, ed., *Site Selection Handbook* (Atlanta: Conway Publications, 1975).

34. Hermone, "The Data You Need to Select a Plant Site," p. 40.

35. Arpan et al., *Directory of Foreign Manufacturers in the United States,* p. xv.

36. See Table 3-2.

37. The word region is herein defined as a group of nearby states.

38. See Table 3-3.

39. These nine regions are: New England, Middle Atlantic, East North Central, West North Central, South Atlantic, East South Central, West South Central, Mountain, and Pacific; U.S. Bureau of the Census, *Census of Manufacturers,* vol. III, pt. 1 (Washington, D.C.: U.S. Government Printing Office, 1976), p. xxxv.

40. See Table 3-1.

41. Russell, *Plant Location,* pp. v and vi.

42. Soderman, *Industrial Location Planning,* p. 5.

43. Speir, "The Common Denominator in Selecting New Sites," p. 30.

44. Letter from Hunter A. Poole, Chief of International Section of North Carolina Department of Commerce, 1 June 1977.

CHAPTER II

1. John C. Clendenin and George A. Christy, *Introduction to Investments,* 5th ed. (New York: McGraw-Hill Book Company, 1969), p. 613.

2. Ibid.

3. U.S., Congress, House, *International Investment Uncertainty,* p. 17.

4. Ibid.

5. U.S. Department of Commerce, *Foreign Direct Investment in the United States* (Washington, D.C.: U.S. Government Printing Office, 1976), 1:xii-3.

6. Before 1974, the official level for a foreign direct investment was a 25 percent ownership. After the passage of Public Law 93-479, the "Foreign Investment Study Act of 1974," the percentage was changed to 10 percent.

7. Webley, *Foreign Direct Investment in the United States: Opportunities and Impediments,* p. 26; "The Multinational Corporation," *Studies on U.S. Foreign Investment,* Vol. 2, U.S. Department of Commerce (Washington, D.C.: U.S. Government Printing Office, 1973); "Multinational Corporations in a Tough New World," *Fortune* (August, 1973), pp. 52-134; Floyd G. Lawrence, "Multinationals Search for One World," *Industry Week,* January 1, 1973, pp. 3-14.

8. Gunnar Beeth, *International Management Practice* (New York: American Management Association, 1973), pp. 1-2.

9. Philip R. Cateora and John M. Hess, *International Marketing* (Homewood, Illinois: Richard D. Irwin, Inc., 1972), p. 8; Peter F. Drucker, "The Rise of Production Sharing," *The Wall Street Journal,* 15 March 1977, p. 16.

10. Webley, *Foreign Direct Investment in the United States: Opportunities and Impediments,* p. 27.

11. Ibid., p. 26.

12. The Conference Board, Inc., *Foreign Investment in the United States: Policy, Problems and Obstacles* (New York: The Conference Board, Inc., 1974), p. 9.

13. U.S., Congress, House, *International Investment Uncertainty,* p. 24.

14. Ibid.

15. Foster, "The Friendly Invasion," p. 27.

16. Daniels, *Recent Foreign Direct Manufacturing Investment in the United States,* pp. 48-56.

17. Soderman, *Industrial Location Planning,* p. 5; David M. Smith, *Industrial Location* (New York: John Wiley and Sons, Inc., 1971), p. 2.

18. George T. Renner, "Geography of Industrial Localization," *Economic Geography,* 1947, p. 169; Smith, *Industrial Location,* p. 99.

19. Renner, "Geography of Industrial Localization," p. 181; Smith, *Industrial Location,* p. 99.

20. Smith, *Industrial Location,* pp. 99-100.

21. Ibid., pp. 100-101.

22. Ibid., p. 103.

23. Ibid., p. 104.

24. Ibid., p. 109.

25. Ibid., pp. 106-107.

26. Johann Heinrich Von Thunen, *Der Isolierte Staat in Beziehung auf Landwirtschaft und Nationalokonomie,* 3rd ed. (Berlin: Schumacher-Zarchlin, 1875); this book has been translated as *The Isolated State.*

27. Donald J. Bowersox, Edward W. Smykay, and Bernard J. La Londe, *Physical Distribution Management* (New York: The Macmillan Company, 1968), p. 69.

28. George M. McManmon, *A Survey of the Literature on Industrial Location* (New York: Business Research Center, Syracuse University, 1959), p. 9.

29. This book has been translated by C.J. Friedrich as *Alfred Weber's Theory of the Location of Industries* (Chicago: University of Chicago Press, 1928); Smith, *Industrial Location,* p. 113.

30. *Alfred Weber's Theory of the Location of Industries* cited in Luther T. Wallace, Jr., "Factors Affecting Industrial Location in Southern Indiana" (Ph.D. dissertation, Purdue University, 1960), pp. 165-66.

31. Bowersox et al., *Physical Distribution Management,* pp. 69-70.

32. Smith, *Industrial Location,* pp. 130-31.

33. *Economics of Location,* cited in Wallace, "Factors Affecting Industrial Location in Southern Indiana," pp. 186-87; William F. Davidge, Jr., "The Attractive Influence and Current Adequacy of Mississippi Industrial Location Factors" (Ph.D. dissertation, The University of Mississippi, 1976), p. 26.

34. Edgar M. Hoover, *Location Theory and the Shoe and Leather Industries* (Cambridge: Harvard University Press, 1937).

35. Idem, *Location of Economic Activity,* 1st ed. (New York: McGraw-Hill Book Company, 1948).

36. *Location of Economic Activity,* cited in Wallace, "Factors Affecting Industrial Location in Southern Indiana," p. 194.

37. Ibid., p. 196.

38. *Location of Economic Activity,* cited in McManmon, *A Survey of the Literature on Industrial Location,* pp. 56-57.

39. Melvin L. Greenhut, *Plant Location in Theory and in Practice* (Chapel Hill, North Carolina: The University of North Carolina Press, 1956), p. 279.

40. Ibid., pp. 279-80.

41. Ibid., p. 280.

42. Ibid., p. 281.

43. Ibid., p. 103; Wallace, "Factors Affecting Industrial Location in Southern Indiana," p. 202.

44. Greenhut, *Plant Location in Theory and in Practice,* p. 103.

45. Ibid., pp. 167-70.

46. Walter Isard, *Location and Space Economy* (Cambridge, Mass.: MIT Press, 1956); Idem, *Methods of Regional Analysis* (Cambridge, Mass.: MIT Press, 1960); Bowersox et al., *Physical Distribution Management,* p. 72.

47. Ibid.

48. *Location and Space Economy,* cited in Wallace, "Factors Affecting Industrial Location in Southern Indiana," pp. 216-17.

49. McManmon, *A Survey of the Literature on Industrial Location,* p. 68; Isard, *Location and Space Economy,* pp. 127-37.

50. Daniels, *Recent Foreign Direct Manufacturing Investment in the United States,* p. 62.

51. Ibid., p. 64.

52. Ibid., p. 66.

53. Arpan et al., *Directory of Foreign Manufacturers in the United States,* p. xiv; Idem, "Foreign Direct Investments in the U.S. and some Attendant Research Problems," *Journal of International Business Studies* 5 (Spring 1974), 1-7.

54. Hans Schollhammer, *Locational Strategies of Multinational Firms* (Los Angeles: Center for International Business, Pepperdine University, 1974), p. 3.

55. Bowersox, *Logistical Management,* pp. 494-99.

56. Ibid., p. 445.

57. Hermone, "The Data You Need to Select a Plant Site," pp. 35-40.

58. Ibid., p. 38.

59. T.E. McMillan, Jr., "Why Manufacturers Choose Plant Locations vs. Determinants of Plant Locations," *Land Economics* 41 (August 1965):239-46.

60. Charles Russell Beaton, Jr., "An Analysis of the Factors Affecting the Manufacturing Location Decision within Orange County, California," *Dissertation Abstract* (January/February 1969):1995-A.

61. Liston, *Site Selection Handbook,* pp. 321-30.

62. *Distribution Worldwide* 75 (December 1976):36-39; Bowersox et al., *Physical Distribution Management,* pp. 447-49.

63. Good, *Plant Location;* Liston, *Site Selection Handbook.*

CHAPTER III

1. See Figure 2-1 and Arpan et al., *Directory of Foreign Manufacturers in the United States,* pp. v and vi.

2. This is consistent with the definition of foreign direct investment currently adopted by the U.S. Department of Commerce; see U.S. Congress, House, *International Investment Uncertainty,* p. 18.

3. Arpan et al., *Directory of Foreign Manufacturers in the United States.*

4. U.S. Department of Commerce, *Foreign Direct Investors in the United States* (Washington, D.C.: U.S. Government Printing Office, 1976).

5. See Appendix A-2 for the letter mailed to the states' economic development agencies for the purpose of compiling the mailing list.

6. See Appendix B-1.

7. See Appendix B-2.

8. See Appendix B-3.

9. See Appendix B-4.

10. These two studies were reviewed in Chapter II.

11. Norman H. Nie, et al., *Statistical Package for the Social Sciences,* 2nd ed. (New York: McGraw-Hill Book Company, 1975), pp. 194-201.

12. See Chapter IV.

13. Nie, et al., *Statistical Package for the Social Sciences,* pp. 194-201.

14. Ibid., pp. 249-64.

15. Gene V. Glass and Julian C. Stanley, *Statistical Methods in Education and Psychology* (Englewood Cliffs, N.J.: Prentice-Hall, Inc., 1970), p. 358.

16. Sanford Labovitz, "Criteria for Selecting a Significance Level: A Note on the Sacredness of .05," *The American Sociologist* 3 (August 1968):220-22.

17. Nie, et al., *Statistical Package for the Social Sciences,* pp. 468-508.

18. See Chapter IV.

19. Nie, et al., *Statistical Package for the Social Sciences,* pp. 194-201.

CHAPTER IV

1. See Table 4-1 for the exact presentation order of these eight countries.

2. See Table 4-2 for the exact presentation order of these 11 product categories.

3. See Table 4-3 for the exact presentation order of the 12 states.

4. See Table 4-4 for the exact presentation order of these three employee-size categories.

5. See Table 4-5 for the exact presentation order of these four foreign-ownership categories.

6. Tom Foster, "The Friendly Invasion," p. 27.

7. William D. Wells and Jagdish N. Sheth, "Factor Analysis in Marketing Research," in David A. Aaker, ed., *Multivariate Analysis in Marketing: Theory and Application* (Belmont, Calif: Wadsworth Publishing Company, Inc., 1971), p. 214.

8. Ibid., p. 224.

9. Ibid., pp. 214-215.

10. The 56 percent is derived by dividing the sum of the eigenvalues by 32, the number of plant location factors.

CHAPTER V

1. Arpan et al., *Directory of Foreign Manufacturers in the United States,* p. xiv.

2. Foster, "The Friendly Invasion," p. 29.

APPENDIX A

LETTERS MAILED TO THE FIFTY STATES' ECONOMIC DEVELOPMENT AGENCIES

APPENDIX A-1
SAMPLE OF THE LETTER USED TO INQUIRE
ABOUT PREVIOUS STUDIES

THE UNIVERSITY OF NEBRASKA—LINCOLN
COLLEGE OF BUSINESS ADMINISTRATION
LINCOLN, NEBRASKA 68588

DEPARTMENT OF MARKETING

May 18, 1977

Dear

　　For my Ph.D. dissertation, I am conducting a nationwide survey
concerning plant location decisions of foreign manufacturers in the U.S.
The major question posed in my study is: what is the relative importance
of various plant location factors in the eyes of these foreign investors?
The purpose is twofold: (1) to supply information useful to eager-to-
grow communities for improving their investment climates; and (2) to
provide an opportunity for foreign manufacturing investors to exchange
their opinions and experiences in choosing U.S. plant locations. If your
department or office has done or is familiar with any research on this
subject, would you please send ma a copy of the study or the name of the
authors, the titles, and the sources of these reports. Thank you very
much for your help.

　　　　　　　　　　　　Sincerely yours,

　　　　　　　　　　　　Hsin-Min Tong

　　　　　　　　　　　　Graduate Research Assistant

APPENDIX A-2
SAMPLE OF THE LETTER USED TO COMPILE THE MAILING LIST

THE UNIVERSITY OF NEBRASKA–LINCOLN
COLLEGE OF BUSINESS ADMINISTRATION
LINCOLN, NEBRASKA 68588

DEPARTMENT OF MARKETING

June 14, 1977

Dear

    For my Ph.D. dissertation, I am conducting a nationwide survey concerning plant location decisions of foreign manufacturers in the U.S. Would you please send me an updated list of foreign manufacturing investments in your state, including the chief executive officer's name, company name, and address. Example of such a list is enclosed for your reference.

    I will send you a summary report of my research as soon as it is available. I sincerely appreciate your assistance.

                  Truly yours,

                  Hsin-Min Tong

                  Graduate Research Assistant

Enclosure

APPENDIX B

QUESTIONNAIRE, COVER LETTERS, AND FOLLOW-UP LETTER USED IN THIS STUDY

APPENDIX B-1
SAMPLE OF THE QUESTIONNAIRE—PAGE 1

College of Business Administration
University of Nebraska–Lincoln
Lincoln, Nebraska 68588

PLANT LOCATION STUDY OF FOREIGN MANUFACTURERS IN THE U.S.

General Instructions:

Please ask an executive who either participated in or has the knowledge of your company's plant location decision(s) in the U.S. to fill out this questionnaire.

(In this study, the term "foreign manufacturers" refers to manufacturing firms which have at least one plant in the U.S. and of whose ownership 10 percent or more belongs to non-Americans.)

The focus of this study deals with choosing a particular community in the U.S. in which to locate a plant. In case your company made several plant location decisions in the past, please refer to the most recent decision.

In the following, please either check (√) an appropriate box or write in short answers for each question. You are welcome to give explanations and comments whenever and wherever you think they are warranted. Thank you.

Section I. Classification Information

1. Has your company ever made a U.S. plant location decision?
   Yes ☐ → Please proceed to answer question No. 3
   No ☐ → Please proceed to answer question No. 2

2. Why hasn't your company made a plant location decision in the U.S.? (After you answer this question, please continue to answer question No. 4 and fill out the rest of the questionnaire as completely as possible.)
   a. Company does no manufacturing in the U.S. ☐
   b. Company bought into an existing firm which owned a plant ☐
   c. Other reasons (please specify): _____
   _____
   _____

3. In what year was the plant location decision made? _____

4. How would you categorize the major product(s) of your plant? (Please check only one.)
   SIC Code
   20 Food and Food Products ☐
   22 Textile Mill Products ☐
   26 Paper and Related Products ☐
   28 Chemicals and Allied Products ☐
   30 Rubber and Plastics ☐
   32 Stone, Clay, Glass and Concrete ☐
   33 Primary Metals ☐
   34 Fabricated Metals Products ☐
   35 Industrial Machinery ☐
   36 Electrical Machinery and Equipment ☐
   37 Transportation Equipment ☐
   38 Measuring, Analyzing and Controlling Equipment ☐
   ___ Other (please specify): _____ ☐

5. About how many employees (all the people who receive salaries or wages on a regular basis) was your plant designed to have when the plant location decision was made? _____

6. In what state is your plant located? _____

7. About what percentage of ownership of your company belongs to non-Americans? _____ %

8. What is the nationality of the principal non-American owner(s) of your company? _____

9. From what source(s) did your company get information in order to decide in which community to locate your plant? (Please check all that were used.)

Other firms	☐	Investment missions	☐
State agencies	☐	Local agencies	☐
U.S. Dept. of Commerce	☐	Outside consultants	☐

   Other sources (please specify): _____

OVER

Section II. Importance of Factors Affecting Plant Location Decisions

Listed below are 32 factors that may influence foreign manufacturers like your company to locate a plant in a particular community in the U.S. Please rate each of these factors on a five-point scale according to their importance when the location decision of your plant was made. Add other factors if you wish.

Scale:

Not At All Important	Slightly Important	Moderately Important	Very Important	Extremely Important
1	2	3	4	5

Factors: Please check (√) one box opposite each factor.

	1	2	3	4	5
1. Nearness to markets within the U.S.					
2. Proximity to export markets (outside the U.S.)					
3. Nearness to home operation					
4. Nearness to operations in a "third country"					
5. Facilities for importing and exporting					
6. Proximity to raw material sources					
7. Proximity to suppliers					
8. Availability of managerial and technical personnel					
9. Availability of skilled labor					
10. Availability of unskilled labor					
11. Salary and wage rates					
12. Labor attitudes					
13. Labor laws					
14. Availability of utilities					
15. Cost of utilities					
16. Availability of transportation services					
17. Cost of transportation services					
18. Availability of suitable plant sites					
19. Cost of suitable land					
20. Cost of construction					
21. Ample space for future expansion					
22. Availability of local capital					
23. Cost of local capital					
24. State tax rates					
25. Local tax rates					
26. Government incentives					
27. Attitudes of government officials					
28. Attitudes of local citizens					
29. Housing facilities					
30. Education facilities					
31. Police and fire protection					
32. Climate					

Other Factors: (please specify and rate)

_____

_____

_____

Thank you very much for your help.
Please return this questionnaire to the
Bureau of Business Research
University of Nebraska–Lincoln
Lincoln, Nebraska 68588

APPENDIX B-2
SAMPLE OF THE DEAN'S COVER LETTER

THE UNIVERSITY OF NEBRASKA–LINCOLN
COLLEGE OF BUSINESS ADMINISTRATION
LINCOLN, NEBRASKA 68588

OFFICE OF THE DEAN

September 1, 1977

Dear Sir:

Mr. Hsin-Min Tong, a graduate research assistant in our college, is conducting a nationwide survey concerning plant location factors of foreign manufacturing investors in the United States.

It is my opinion that the findings from Mr. Tong's study would enable communities that desire to attract and keep foreign industrial plants to strengthen and emphasize their real advantages and to eliminate particular disadvantages. I believe, therefore, that your cooperation will be in both American public interest and your company's own interest.

Your assistance in this research by filling out the enclosed questionnaire is essential to the success of his study, and will be greatly appreciated.

Sincerely,

Gary Schwendiman
Interim Dean

THE UNIVERSITY OF NEBRASKA–LINCOLN   THE UNIVERSITY OF NEBRASKA AT OMAHA
THE UNIVERSITY OF NEBRASKA MEDICAL CENTER

APPENDIX B-3
SAMPLE OF THE AUTHOR'S COVER LETTER

THE UNIVERSITY OF NEBRASKA-LINCOLN
COLLEGE OF BUSINESS ADMINISTRATION
LINCOLN. NEBRASKA 68588

DEPARTMENT OF MARKETING

September 1, 1977

Dear

The primary objectives of this study are twofold: (1) to supply useful information to eager-to-grow communities for improving their investment climates; and (2) to provide an opportunity for foreign manufacturing investors in the U.S. to exchange their opinions and experiences of choosing plant locations in the U.S. The findings of this study will be valuable to various U.S. economic development organizations and to foreign manufacturing investors, including your company.

Your company has been selected from the Directory of Foreign Manufacturers in the U.S. Your assistance is extremely important and will be greatly appreciated. All the data supplied by your company will be treated as confidential material; it will be combined with other firms' data and reported only in the form of statistical summaries. Special attention will be paid to make sure that the identification of any individual company is absolutely impossible.

I will send you a summary report of this research free of charge if you complete the enclosed mailing label.

Please return the completed questionnaire at your earliest convenience in the enclosed business reply envelope. If you have any questions, please call me at 402-472-3384. Thank you for your cooperation.

Sincerely,

Hsin-Min Tong
Graduate Research Assistant

Enclosures

THE UNIVERSITY OF NEBRASKA-LINCOLN   THE UNIVERSITY OF NEBRASKA AT OMAHA
THE UNIVERSITY OF NEBRASKA MEDICAL CENTER

APPENDIX B-4
SAMPLE OF THE FOLLOW-UP LETTER

THE UNIVERSITY OF NEBRASKA—LINCOLN
COLLEGE OF BUSINESS ADMINISTRATION
LINCOLN, NEBRASKA 68588

DEPARTMENT OF MARKETING

September 22, 1977

Dear

    Three weeks ago I mailed to you a "Plant Location Study of Foreign Manufacturers in the U.S." questionnaire from the University of Nebraska-Lincoln. So far, the response rate has been very encouraging, but several firms have not replied yet. Since all returns are held in strict confidence, I am unable to distinguish between those that have responded from those that have not.

    In the event that you have already completed the questionnaire and forwarded it to me, I sincerely appreciate your cooperation (and just throw away this extra copy). However, if you inadvertently placed the questionnaire aside, or postponed answering it for a few days, I would like to encourage you to forward the requested information as soon as possible.

    Your help is essential and necessary to the success of this study. I appreciate your early response. If you have any questions or need any additional information, please call me at 402-472-3384. Thank you.

Truly yours,

Hsin-Min Tong
Graduate Research Assistant

Enclosures

SELECTED BIBLIOGRAPHY

BOOKS

Aharoni, Yair. *The Foreign Investment Decision Process.* Boston: Graduate School of Business Administration, Harvard University, 1966.

Arkin, Herbert. *Handbook of Sampling for Auditing and Accounting.* New York: McGraw-Hill Book Company, 1974.

Arpan, Jeffrey S., and Ricks, David A. *Directory of Foreign Manufacturers in the United States.* Atlanta: School of Business Administration, Georgia State University, 1975.

Beckmann, Martin. *Location Theory.* New York: Random House, Inc., 1968.

Beeth, Gunnar. *International Management Practice.* New York: American Management Association, 1973.

Blackett, Olin W. *Water Resources and Plant Location in Michigan.* Ann Arbor: School of Business Administration, University of Michigan, 1957.

Bowersox, Donald J. *Logistical Management.* New York: Macmillan Publishing Co., Inc., 1974.

Bowersox, Donald J.; Smykay, Edward W.; and La Londe, Bernard J. *Physical Distribution Management.* New York: The Macmillan Company, 1968.

British Institute of Management. *Overseas Investment.* London: British Institute of Management, 1968.

Buchanan, Norman S. *International Investment and Domestic Welfare.* New York: Henry Holt and Company, Inc., 1945.

Cassel, Gustav; Gregory, Theodor E.; Kuczynski, Robert E.; and Norton, Henry Kittredge. *Foreign Investments.* Chicago: The University of Chicago Press, 1928.

Cateora, Philip R., and Hess, John M. *International Marketing.* Homewood, Ill.: Richard D. Irwin, Inc., 1972.

Clendenin, John C., and Christy, George A. *Introduction to Investments.* New York: McGraw-Hill Book Company, 1969.

Colebrook, Philip. *Going International.* London: McGraw-Hill Book Company (UK) Limited, 1972.

The Conference Board, Inc., *Foreign Investment in the United States: Policy, Problems and Obstacles.* New York: The Conference Board, Inc., 1974.

Daniels, John D. *Recent Foreign Direct Manufacturing Investment in the United States.* New York: Praeger Publishers, Inc., 1971.

Davies, A. Emil. *Investments Abroad.* Chicago: A.W. Shaw Company, 1927.

Dixon, Brian. *The St. Lawrence Seaway and the Connecting Channels: Their Influence on Plant Location in Michigan.* Ann Arbor: School of Business Administration, University of Michigan, 1957.

Dougall, Herbert E. *Investments.* 9th ed. Englewood Cliffs, N.J.: Prentice-Hall, Inc., 1973.

Dunning, John H. *Studies in International Investment.* London: George Allen & Unwin Ltd., 1970.

Estall, R.C., and Buchanan, R. Ogilvie. *Industrial Activity and Economic Geography.* London: Hutchinson & Co. Ltd., 1973.

Faith, Nicholas. *The Infiltrators.* London: Hamish Hamilton Ltd., 1971.

Francis, Jack Clark. *Investments: Analysis and Management.* New York: McGraw-Hill Book Company, 1976.

Glass, Gene V., and Stanley, Julian C. *Statistical Methods in Educaion and Psychology.* Englewood Cliffs, N.J.: Prentice-Hall, Inc., 1970.

Gray, H. Peter. *The Economics of Business Investment Abroad.* London: The Macmillan Press Ltd., 1972.

Greene, Walter E. *Plant Location Factors.* Chicago: Adams Press, 1969.

Greenhut, Melvin L. *Plant Location in Theory and in Practice.* Chapel Hill, N.C.: The University of North Carolina Press, 1956.

_____. *Microeconomics and the Space Economy.* Chicago: Scott, Foresman and Company, 1963.

_____. *A Theory of the Firm in Economic Space.* New York: Appleton-Century-Crofts, 1970.

Hellman, Rainer. *The Challenge to U.S. Dominance of the International Corporation,* trans. Peter Ruof. New York: Dunellen Publishing Company, Inc., 1970.

Hoover, Edgar M. *Location Theory and the Shoe and Leather Industry.* Cambridge: The Harvard University Press, 1937.

_____. *An Introduction to Regional Economics.* New York: Alfred A. Knopf, 1971.

Hymer, Stephen Herbert. *The International Operations of National Firms: A Study of Direct Foreign Investment.* Cambridge, Massachusetts: The MIT Press, 1976.

Isard, Walter. *Location and Space-Economy.* New York: The MIT Press, 1956.

_____. *Methods of Regional Analysis: An Introduction to Regional Science.* New York: The Technology Press of the Massachusetts Institute of Technology, John Wiley and Sons, Inc., 1960.

Isard, Walter, and Smith, Tony. *General Theory: Social, Political, Economic, and Regional.* Cambridge, Mass: The MIT Press, 1969.

Kemp, Murray C. *The Pure Theory of International Trade and Investment.* Englewood Cliffs, N.J.: Prentice-Hall, Inc., 1969.

_____. *Three Topics in the Theory of International Trade.* New York: American Elsevier Publishing Company, Inc., 1976.

Kotler, Philip. *Marketing Management.* 2nd ed. Englewood Cliffs, N.J.: Prentice-Hall, Inc., 1972.

Lishan, John M., and Crary, David T. *The Investment Process.* Scranton, Pa.: International Textbook Company, 1970.

Lösch, August. *The Economics of Location.* New Haven, Conn.: Yale University Press, 1954.

McManmon, George M. *A Survey of the Literature on Industrial Location.* New York: Business Research Center, Syracuse University, 1959.

Mandell, Lewis. *Industrial Location Decisions.* New York: Praeger Publishers, Inc., 1975.

Miller, E. Willard. *A Geography of Industrial Location.* Dubuque, Iowa: Wm. C. Brown Company Publishers, 1970.

Milne, Robert D., ed. *Investment Values in a Dynamic World: The Collected Papers of Nicholas Molodovsky.* Homewood, Ill.: Richard D. Irwin, Inc., 1974.

Nie, Norman H.; Hull, C. Hadlai; Jenkins, Jean G.: Steinbrenner, Karin; and Bent, Dale H. *Statistical Package for the Social Sciences.* New York: McGraw-Hill Book Company, 1975.

Otterbeck, Lars. *Location and Strategic Planning-Towards a Contingency Theory of Industrial Location.* Stockholm: The Economic Research Institute at the Stockholm School of Economics, 1973.

Rippy, J. Fred. *British Investments in Latin America, 1822-1949.* Minneapolis: University of Minnesota Press, 1959.

The Royal Institute of International Affairs. *The Problem of International Investment.* London: Oxford University Press, 1937.

Russell, Joseph A. *Plant Location.* New York: American Research Council, Inc., 1956.

Schollhammer, Hans. *Locational Strategies of Multinational Firms.* Los Angeles: Center for International Business, Pepperdine University, 1974.

Smith, David M. *Industrial Location.* New York: John Wiley and Sons, Inc., 1971.

Soderman, Sten. *Industrial Location Planning.* Stockholm: Almqvist and Wiksell International, 1975.

Staley, Eugene. *War and the Private Investor—A Study in the Relations of International Politics and International Private Investment.* Garden City, N.Y.: Doubleday, Doran and Company, Inc., 1935.

Thompson, James H. *Methods of Plant Site Selection Available to Small Manufacturing Firms.* Bureau of Business Research, West Virginia University, 1961.

Townroe, Peter M. *Industrial Location Decisions.* London: Research Publications Services Ltd., 1971.

———. *Planning Industrial Location.* London: Leonard Hill Books, 1976.

U.S. Congress, House. *International Investment Uncertainty.* 94th Cong., 2nd sess. Washington D.C.: U.S. Government Printing Office, 1977.

U.S. Department of Commerce, Office of Business Economics, *Foreign Business Investments in the United States.* Washington D.C.: U.S. Government Printing Office, 1962.

Von Thünen, Johann M. *Der Isoberte Staat in Bejiehung auf Landwirtschaft und Nationalokonomie.* 3rd ed. trans. Peter Hall. Berlin: Schuwacherzarcklin, 1875.

Weber, Alfred. *Theory of the Location of Industries.* trans. C.J. Friedrich. Chicago: University of Chicago Press, 1929.

Webley, Simon. *Foreign Direct Investment in the United States: Opportunities and Impediments.* London: British-North American Committee, 1974.

Yaseen, Leonard C. *Plant Location.* Roslyn, N.Y.: Business Reports, Inc., 1952.

_____ . *Plant Location.* New York: American Research Council, 1956.

ARTICLES

Albert, Linzy D., and Kellow, James H. "Decision-Makers' Reactions to Plant Location Factors: An Appraisal." *Land Economics* 45 (August 1969):376-81.

Alexander, J.W. "Location of Manufacturing: Methods of Measurement." *Annals,* Association of American Geographers, 48 (1958):20-26.

Atkins, Robert J., and Shriver, Richard H. "New Approach to Facilities Location." *Harvard Business Review* 36 (May-June 1968):70-79.

Ballabon, M.B. "Putting the 'Economics' into Economic Geography." *Economic Geography* 33 (1957):217-223.

Boventer, E. Von. "The Relationship Between Transportation Costs and Location Rent in Transportation Problems." *Journal of Regional Science* 3 (1961):27-40.

Bridges, B. "State and Local Inducements for Industry." *National Tax Journal* 18 (1965): 1-14 and 175-92.

Carrier, Ronald E., and Schriver, William R. "Location Theory: An Empirical Model and Selected Findings." *Land Economics* 44 (November 1968):450-460.

Drucker, Peter F. "The Rise of Production Sharing." *The Wall Street Journal,* 15 March 1977, p. 16.

Foster, Tom. "The Friendly Invasion." *Distribution Worldwide* 75 (December 1976):27-43.

Fuchs, V.R. "The Determinants of the Redistribution of Manufacturing in the United States Since 1929." *Review of Economics and Statistics* 44 (1962):167-77.

Fulton, M. "Plant Location—1965." *Harvard Business Review* 33 (1955):40-50.

Fulton, M. "Where to Locate Your Plant." *American Machinist/Metalworking Manufacturing* (December 1960):121-128.

Fulton, M., and Hoch, L.C. "Transportation Factors Affecting Locational Decisions." *Economic Geography* 35 (1959):51-59.

Greenhut, M.L. "Observations of Motives to Industrial Location." *Southern Economic Journal* 18 (1951):225-28.

_____ . "Size of Market vs. Transport Costs in Industrial Location Survey and Theory." *Journal of Industrial Economics* 8 (1960):172-84.

_____ . "When is the Demand Factor of Location Important?" *Land Economics* 40 (1964):175-84.

Hermone, Ronald H. "The Data You Need to Select a Plant Site." *Management Review* 59 (November 1970):35-40.

Hoover, E.M. "The Measurement of Industrial Localization." *Review of Economics and Statistics* 18 (1936):162-71.

Isard, W., and Schooler, E.W. "Industrial Complex Analysis, Agglomeration Economies and Regional Development." *Journal of Regional Science* 1 (1959):19-33.

"Japanese Firm Will Build Plant in U.S., Make Color TV Sets." *Lincoln Morning Journal*, 1 April 1977, sec. 1, p. 1.

Lawrence, Floyd G. "Multinationals Search for One World." *Industrial Week* (January 1, 1973):3-14.

Leontief, W. W. "The Structure of the U.S. Economy." *Scientific American* 212 (1965): 25-35.

Lloyd, P.E., and Dicken, P. "The Data Bank in Regional Studies of Industry." *Town Planning Review* 38 (1968):304-16.

McMillan, T.E., Jr. "Why Manufacturers Choose Plant Locations vs. Determinants of Plant Locations." *Land Economics* 41 (August 1965):239-46.

Nishioka, Hisao, and Krumme, Gunter. "Location Conditions, Factors and Decisions; An Evaluation of Selected Location Surveys." *Land Economics* 49 (May 1973):195-205.

"Plant Site Selection: Just One Constant Factor." *The Magazine of Wall Street* Vol. 124, No. 10, August 16, 1969, p. 17 and 47.

Renner, G.T. "Geography of Industrial Localization." *Economic Geography* 23 (1947): 167-89.

Renner, G.T. "Some Principles and Laws of Economic Geography." *Journal of Geography* 49 (1950):14-22.

Smith, D.M. "A Theoretical Framework for Geographical Studies of Industrial Location." *Economic Geography* 42 (1966):95-113.

Speir, William B. "The Common Denominator in Selecting New Sites." *Industrial Development and Manufacturers Record* 138 (January/February 1969):30-32.

Voorhees, Roy D. "Communications: A New Logistics Factor in Location Decisions and Patterns of Regional and National Development." *Transportation Journal* 15 (Summer 1976): 73-84.

Wood, P. "Industrial Location and Linkage." *Area* No. 2 (1969):32-39.

DISSERTATIONS

Davidge, William Frederick, Jr. "The Attractive Influence and Current Adequacy of Mississippi Industrial Location Factors, 1963-1972," Ph.D. dissertation, University of Mississippi, 1976.

Hanline, Manning Harold. "Decision-Making and Industrial Location in the Southwest, 1946-1961." Ph.D. dissertation, the Ohio State University, 1965.

Scheer, Lorraine H. "Influence of Location Factors in the Tulsa Area Plant Location Decision, 1958-1969." Ph.D. dissertation, University of Oklahoma, 1971.

Wallace, Luther Tompkins, Jr. "Factors Affecting Industrial Location in Southern Indiana." Ph.D. dissertation, Purdue University, 1960.

INDEX

Oil Production and Export Cartel (OPEC) nations, 15
Outward foreign investment, 15

Physical restriction, principle of, 21
Plant analysis, 8
Plant location decision, 9; behavioral matrix, 21; communication sources, 9; community level, 8; confirmation of, 9; importance of, 3, 12; institutional factors, 23; maximum profit as the criterion, 23; personal factors, 25; regional level, 8; site level, 8
Plant-location-decision process: model of, 6; stages of, 6
Plant location factors: basic dimensions underlying, 52; importance of, for all respondents, 44; importance of, by employee-size categories, 49; importance of, by foreign-ownership categories, 50; importance of, by major investing countries, 45; importance of, by major product categories, 46; importance of, by major states, 48; list of, 32, 119; meaning of, 9
Poole, Hunder A., 12
Population and frame, 33
Pred, Allen, 21
Pretest, 36
Public Law 93-479, 15

Questionnaire, design of, 34

Rawstron, E.M., 21
Regional science, 26

Renner, George, 20
Response rate, 39
Reverse investment, 15
Ricks, David A., 9, 28, 39
Russell, Joseph A., 12

Schollhammer, Hans, 28
Site selections, checklist of, 30
Soderman, Sten, 12
Speir, William B., 12
Statistical Package for the Social Sciences (SPSS): "Breakdown" subprogram, 40; "Factor" subprogram, 40; "Frequencies" subprogram, 39
Stoetzel, Jean, 4
Substitution principle, 26

Technical restriction, principle of, 21
Toshiba, 6
Transportation costs, 6

Ullman, E.L., 20
Unusuable returns, 39
U.S. dollar, devaluation of, 6
U.S. tariffs, 6

Von Thunen, Johan Henrich, 22

Weber, Alfred, 22
Webley, Simon, 5
Williams, Frederick, 4
Wilton, Peter, 6

Xenophobia, 15